The Gardener's Guide to Plant Conservation

World Wildlife Fund

World Wildlife Fund (WWF) is the largest private U.S. conservation organization working worldwide to conserve nature. WWF works to preserve the diversity and abundance of life on Earth and the health of ecological systems by protecting natural areas and wildlife populations, promoting sustainable use of natural resources, and promoting more efficient resource and energy use and the maximum reduction of pollution. WWF is affiliated with the international WWF network, which has national organizations, associates, or representatives in nearly 40 countries. In the United States, WWF has more than 1 million members.

The Garden Club of America

The Garden Club of America is a national association of garden clubs working together to promote horticulture and the preservation of the environment on the local and national level through conservation education, scholarship programs, publications, historic preservation, civic beautification, and flower shows. Founded in 1913, the Garden Club of America has over 15,000 members in 189 garden clubs located in 38 states and the District of Columbia.

TRAFFIC USA

TRAFFIC USA is the United States affiliate of the international TRAFFIC network, a joint program of World Wildlife Fund and the World Conservation Union (IUCN). With 17 offices worldwide, TRAFFIC monitors the global trade in wildlife and wildlife products through research, reports, investigations, and scientific analysis. TRAFFIC USA is the principal source in the United States for objective information on international wildlife trade for the U.S. government, nongovernmental organizations, and industry.

The Gardener's Guide to Plant Conservation

by Nina T. Marshall

World Wildlife Fund
Washington, D.C.

Book orders should be directed to World Wildlife Fund,
P.O. Box 4866, Hampden Post Office, Baltimore, MD 21211.
Telephone (410) 516-6951.

The Gardener's Guide to Plant Conservation

Cover photo: *Erythronium californicum*, by Nina Marshall.
Design by Rings Leighton Limited, Washington, D.C.
Printed by Automated Graphics Systems, White Plains, Maryland.
10 9 8 7 6 5 4 3 2 1

Library of Congress Cataloging-in-Publication Data
The Gardener's guide to plant conservation.
p. cm.
Includes bibliographical references.
ISBN 0-89164-139-4 : $12.95
1. Plant conservation–United States. 2. Plant conservation. 3. Wild flowers–United States. 4. Endangered plants–United States. 5. Plants, Ornamental–United States. 6. Wild flower gardening–United States. I. World Wildlife Fund (U.S.) II. Garden Club of America.
QK86.U6G355 1993
693.9'9--dc20 92-42403
CIP

Printed on recycled paper using vegetable-based inks.

Dedicated to M. H. S. A.

For her generosity of time and spirit and her unwavering commitment to the preservation of Earth's endangered flora.

Contents

Foreword

During the early 1980s, a number of conservation groups and individuals became concerned about the quantity of wild-collected bulbs and wildflowers regularly appearing in North American and European markets but could find little information about this trade. In response, three groups in the United States, World Wildlife Fund (WWF), The Garden Club of America (GCA), and the Natural Resources Defense Council (NRDC), collaborated on research to determine the species and origins of bulbs and wildflowers appearing in trade.

A ground-breaking report prepared by Sara Oldfield for WWF in 1989 showed not only that trade in wild plants is substantial but also that many of the species in trade are threatened or endangered. Out of this realization, *The Gardener's Guide to Plant Conservation* was born. Dr. Faith Campbell of NRDC conceived of a popular guide publicizing information about the status of wild-collected bulbs and wildflowers in trade, and GCA and WWF set about making the guide a reality. Nina Marshall of TRAFFIC USA, the WWF wildlife trade monitoring program, took on the challenge of transforming and expanding Sara Oldfield's technical report into a book geared toward the general gardening public.

We are pleased to present this final product from two organizations that share a concern about the disappearance of plants from the wild. Broad public education is a critical component in the plant conservation effort. It is our hope that this book will find its way to gardeners and conservationists across North America and will create an awareness leading toward a new ethic in gardening.

—Kathryn S. Fuller
President
World Wildlife Fund
Washington, D.C.

—Nancy S. Thomas
President
The Garden Club of America
New York, N.Y.

Acknowledgments

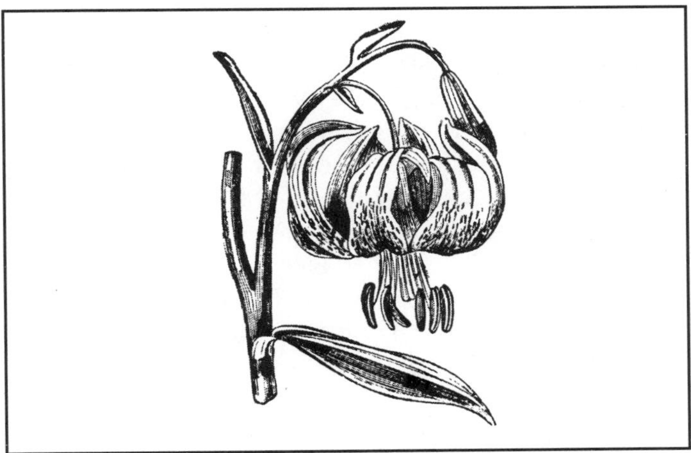

I owe the foundation of this book to Sara Oldfield, whose *Bulb Propagation and Trade Study–Phase II* has had a profound influence on so many of the following pages. Her original research, as well as her encouragement, has been invaluable. Judy Sellers also deserves an enormous thank you for her contribution. Judy not only provided constant assistance and inspiration, but also carried out the primary research for the chapter on North American Wildflowers. Without her assistance and expertise, this chapter as well as many other sections of the book would simply not exist.

Thanks are also due to my constant companions in bulb work. Faith Campbell provided daily encouragement, and kept me going with her determination, enthusiasm, and passion for the plant kingdom. Mike Read, from across the Atlantic, provided excellent insight into the bulb trade, with a sense of humor that provoked smile after smile. But most of all, I must thank Marjorie Arundel, whose dedication to the cause fueled my efforts from start to finish. Her continual quest for information and the endless energy she put into discussions, debate, and deliberations on bulb and native wildflower issues gave me the inspiration to get through even the most difficult parts of this project.

Thanks are also due to the many people who assisted in research, reviewed draft text, or contributed in many other ways. I am particularly grateful to Robert Bogers, Eric Breed, William Brumback, Deb Callister, Coralie Clement, Pam Cubberly, Diane Dalton, Ron Determan, Philip Eckersley, Vonda Frantz, Madeleine Groves, Patti Hagan, Becky Heath, Brent Heath, John Hummer, Mimi Hutchins, Benson Kirkman, Arnold van Kreveld, Ashok Kumar, Ann Lacklen, Mary Margaret Ledbetter, Jessie Lee, Bruce MacBryde, Jane MacKnight, Mimi Marshall, Brian Mathew, Timothy Mayhew, Jeff McCormack, Noel McGough, Linda McMahan, Teresa Mulliken, David Newton, Kristin Nowell, Linda Paine, Brad Rymph, Gordon Smith, William Steele, Martine Todisco, Erick Toledo, James Waddick, Bruce Weissgold, Henk Westerhof, and Louise Wrinkle.

I am also indebted to Kathryn Fuller, president of World Wildlife Fund, and to Jim Leape, senior vice president, and especially to four people who put up with me on a daily basis throughout the long ordeal. During the ups and downs, they listened to my complaints and shared my enthusiasm. To all the staff at TRAFFIC USA—Holly Reed, Andrea Gaski, Ginette Hemley, and Kurt Johnson—your excellent technical advice, friendship, and, of course, your practical jokes, will always be dear to my heart.

I also sincerely appreciate the guidance and encouragement of Bob McCoy, senior editor at WWF. Bob ushered this work through every stage from manuscript to final product; his enthusiasm and expertise were invaluable. To Allison Rogers and David Martin, I am also particularly grateful. Through their creativity and hard work, the manuscript was transformed from mere text into the product you see before you.

Finally, a heartfelt thank you goes to my grandfather, John H. Marshall, who believed in my work and helped me to acquire the essential research materials without which this book would never have been finished. And last, but most of all, endless thanks go to Jared Crawford for listening, for laughing, and for always being there.

Author's Note

The Gardener's Guide to Plant Conservation is designed as a resource for the North American gardening community. The guide was not written for taxonomists; taxonomic difficulties prevail in many genera, and it is not the aim of this work to try to decipher what the experts in the field cannot agree on. Nor did I write for the horticultural specialist seeking the last word on a species or genus. The species found on the following pages have been compiled from nursery catalogs distributed over the last several years. The lists do not include every wildflower or bulb sold in the United States, but instead focus on those species most frequently available to the American gardener. As roadside stands were not surveyed, gardeners may find that some species they are familiar with are not reviewed here. Likewise, stock featured by some specialist nurseries may be absent, simply because I did not attempt to review every nursery catalog in the United States.

It is important to realize that the information presented here is changing and will continue to change in the future. This is a first step in providing much-needed information to gardeners, who are becoming increasingly interested in conservation issues. I hope it will inspire and encourage others to conduct research on plant conservation, propagation, trade, and management and will raise public awareness about endangered species.

Part I

Introduction

Each year, gardeners across the United States buy bulbs and native wildflowers that have been collected from natural areas on every continent except Antarctica. Although many American gardens are dominated by large, dazzling flowers, most of which reflect centuries of expert hybridizing by horticulturists, gardeners are also attracted to the petite elegance of original species, or "botanicals" as they are frequently called. While many of these botanicals are cultivated in nurseries in Europe and the United States, some of the delicate species — for example, *Narcissus* and glory of the snow (*Chionodoxa*) — hail from such exotic locales as the hills of northern Spain or the mountains of southwestern Turkey.

Despite their remote origins, these plants are not thought of as unusual additions to our flowerbeds. Rather, they have been commonplace for decades. In many cases, we have become so accustomed to their appearance that we think of them as natives. Spring would seem incomplete if we couldn't look out the window and see snowdrops, winter aconites, and scillas. Yet these species are not American; they have their origins in southern

Europe and southwestern Asia. The giant snowdrop, *Galanthus elwesii*, distributed throughout southeastern Europe and Turkey, is collected in enormous quantities, especially in the mountainous regions of northern and southwestern Turkey. During the 1988-1989 commercial year, the Netherlands imported from Turkey over 26 million bulbs of the genus *Galanthus*, most of which were the giant snowdrop. These plants are now becoming scarce in certain areas as collection pressures combine with grazing to reduce plant populations.

The problem of plants disappearing from the wild is not confined to foreign lands. Americans have enjoyed collecting native bulbs and wildflowers from woodlands or meadows for centuries. *Trillium*, a popular plant in American woodland gardens, is dug from forested areas in the United States and Canada. Sought by avid gardeners because of its classic blossom and distinctive leaves, *Trillium* is regularly available in retail centers and through mail-order operations. *Trillium*, *Arisaema*, and many other genera are also collected in substantial numbers for export to Europe.

Should we, the American gardening public, be concerned that wild-collected plants are widely available on the U.S. horticultural market? While we enrich our gardens, are wild plant populations becoming depleted or even disappearing entirely? If someone walking in a cool, shady forest fails to come across a carpet of white-blossomed *Trillium*, will the world be a lesser place?

The decade of the 1990s seems to be signaling a more environmentally aware lifestyle for many Americans. Increasingly, people are thinking about issues such as recycling, proper disposal of chemicals, and protection of natural areas. Some contemporary garden writers are encouraging us to appreciate nature through cultivation of native wildflowers. As conscientious gardeners, however, it is our responsibility to be aware of and to understand conservation issues that involve both native and exotic plant species. Our "appreciation" of nature by purchasing wild plants may, ironically, contribute to nature's degradation.

The Gardener's Guide to Plant Conservation was written to assist American gardeners in making choices about the plants they buy for their gardens. The plant species examined are those that a gardener living in the temperate zone in the United States might consider purchasing. The guide includes discussions of issues pertaining to the collection of plants from the wild and general guidelines for gardeners, as well as reference charts indicating the likely origin of popular plant species. There are four reference chapters: native North American wildflowers, bulbs, insectivorous plants, and terrestrial orchids. Each of these chapters lists the plants commonly available to U. S. gardeners and categorizes the origin of each species as either wild-collected, artificially propagated, or a combination of both. Following these lists is a section on sources of information that gardeners can consult for assistance, as well as a glossary and bibliography.

I.

Wild Plants in Trade

In the United States, interest in lawn and garden care climbed dramatically during the 1980s, with gardening purchases reaching $2.6 billion in 1989. Of that total, $470 million was spent for flower bulbs alone. Over one billion bulbs are now purchased in the United States each year, an increase of 450 million bulbs since 1982.

An estimated 35 million people in the United States tend flower gardens, and their gardens vary greatly with the region and climate. Homeowners in the Southwest, for example, are likely to landscape their yards with cacti and other drought-resistant shrubs, ground covers, and flowers. In moister frost-free areas, gardeners cultivate tropical plants such as palms, ferns, cycads, and aroids.

These gardeners might be surprised to learn how many beautiful pictures in gardening catalogs are of plants collected from the wild. Somehow, the catalogs' well-framed photographs, elegant drawings, and enticing descriptions impart a sense of commitment from the nursery to time, quality, and caring. And, in many instances, this is indeed the case. Thousands of commercial growers in Europe raise bulbs from seed or vegetatively, and countless nurseries in the United States are dedicated to propagating the plants they sell. These horticulturists devote energy and expertise to producing top-quality plants that are healthy and free of disease.

Still, aside from those gardeners who venture out into the woods and meadows to collect plants for their own gardens, few people are likely to realize how many commercially available plant species are of wild origin. Most gardeners purchase native species, such as the adder's tongue, white clintonia, and meadow lily, and imports such as *Cyclamen* and the winter daffodil (*Sternbergia*), in local garden centers and from speciality mail-order catalogs. Gardeners usually are unaware when purchasing these plants that often they have been collected from the wild.

The reasons for the existence of wild plants in the horticultural trade are complex and numerous. They are rooted in history and perpetuated by modern realities.

Why Do Wild Plants Appear in Trade?

Although the presence of wild plants in trade has only recently become an issue of concern in conservation and gardening circles, the phenomenon is not new. For thousands of years, people have obtained and cultivated plants, not only for their nutritional, medicinal, and practical benefits but also for their novelty and beauty. As early as the third millennium B.C., the Egyptians were gathering gums and resins from desert shrubs for use in perfumes and medicine and as incense. Exotic plants often reached new lands by way of the ancient spice trade routes, such as the Incense Route stretching from Arabia to Egypt and Syria, and the Silk Road, which linked cities along the Mediterranean with the spice markets of India.

As Turkish influence extended into western Europe in the 15th and 16th centuries, the volume of plants in trade began to increase dramatically. With the employment of the French botanist Clusius (1526-1609) by Emperor Ferdinand I of Vienna, western Europe began an era of unprecedented bulb introduction and cultivation. The Netherlands soon became the world's most prominent commercial center for bulb growing, a position it holds to this day.

As bulbs were increasing in popularity, other types of plants were also being introduced to Europe. Economic prosperity and significant advances in sailing vessel construction allowed Europeans to reach almost every part of the globe. Explorers returned with specimens of orchids, palms, ferns, cacti and succulents, many never before seen on the continent. Initially, study and cultivation of these exotic plants was undertaken only by scientists at botanical gardens, universities, and other institutions and by the occasional wealthy amateur who could afford what was then an extremely costly hobby. By the 17th and 18th centuries, faster and less expensive modes of transportation, as well as improved techniques to transport live plants over long distances, sparked a substantial expansion of commercial trade in ornamental species. Collectors began to exploit wild plant populations as never before.

During the Victorian era, cacti, bulbs, orchids, and other novel plants became economically accessible to and popular with the growing middle classes of Europe and North America. Nature was a central theme in the Victorian lifestyle, and many households became showcases of greenery. Conservatories harboring lilies from the Himalayas, acacias from the Orient, and bromeliads from the Amazon were extremely popular. Some gardeners even went so far as to create miniature tropical forests complete with cashew, banana, mango, and breadfruit trees.

Prior to the 20th century, few Westerners concerned themselves with the impact of trade on wild plant populations. Exotic flora created enormous excitement among those with the means to tend greenhouses and specialty gardens and also yielded huge profits for those who clamored to satisfy that demand.

Today, many of the novelty plants of the past have become standard garden choices; yet some continue to come from wild sources. Consumers of wild plants are ordinary gardeners who take advantage of advertised specials on bulbs, native wildflowers, and other plant groups. In recent years, gardeners have become interested in species bulbs (nonhybrid, that is) and wildflowers; these plants are beautiful, delicate, elegant, and often miniature, just the attributes that seem to be coming into style in the United States. In most cases, few clues exist to notify consumers that their plant selections are of wild origin, except that they seem like a bargain. With this new demand, gardeners and conservationists alike have become concerned about the fate of wild plant populations.

Commercial Collection

Commercial collection as a specific cause of habitat loss and species depletion is particularly pernicious for several reasons. Most important, commercial collection tends to be selective. Cost-effective collection cannot involve the random gathering of plants that the collector happens to come across. Instead, individual species must be targeted, and an area searched with the objective of collecting as many individual plants of the species as possible. In some cases, collectors may practice conservation measures to increase the likelihood that a plant population recovers, such as restricting collection to mature individuals or allowing portions of the population to remain untouched. Numerous collectors, however, harvest an entire population, leaving the future of the plant species in that location uncertain.

The problems stemming from selective collection are exacerbated by the harvest of plants during inappropriate stages of their life cycle. For example, many bulb species are collected when they are in bloom, because they are difficult to identify by their leaves alone. This practice causes added stress, largely because the plant is channeling its energy into flower production rather than coping with loss of soil, water, and sunlight. Also important, collection during flowering eliminates any possibility of seed set. Because no seeds are produced in the collection year, regeneration of the species is greatly reduced. In this manner, plant populations can be rapidly depleted.

What Is a Propagated Plant?

In recent years, there has been some argument about what constitutes true propagation and what is truly of wild origin. For bulbs, the discussion has focused largely on the genus *Galanthus*. In Turkey, it is common practice for villagers to collect wild bulbs of this genus. Bulbs that are too small to export are transplanted to growing fields and subsequently marketed as propagated plants. However, because the growing stock must be continually replaced by wild plants, the time between collection and export is irrelevant. These bulbs originated as wild bulbs, and wild bulbs they remain, no matter how long they sit in the transplant fields.

Throughout this guide, plants defined as "propagated" fall under the definition used by the Convention on International Trade in Endangered Species of Wild Fauna and Flora (CITES), the international treaty regulating wildlife trade. According to CITES

i) the term "artificially propagated" shall be interpreted to refer only to plants grown from seeds, cuttings, divisions, callus tissues or other plant tissues, spores, or other propagules under controlled conditions;

"under controlled conditions" means in a non-natural environment that is intensively manipulated by human intervention for the purpose of producing selected species or hybrids. General characteristics of controlled conditions may include but are not limited to tillage, fertilization, weed control, irrigation, or nursery operations such as potting, bedding, or protection from weather;

ii) the cultivated parental stock used for artificial propagation must be:

A) established and maintained in a manner not detrimental to the survival of the species in the wild; and

B) managed in such a way that long-term maintenance of this cultivated stock is guaranteed; and

iii) grafted plants shall be recognized as artificially propagated only when both the root-stock and the graft have been artificially propagated; ...

This definition has been adopted by the member nations of CITES. (Further information about the treaty is contained in chapter 2.)

Persistence of Wild Collection

Propagation activities have increased dramatically in recent decades, helping to rescue many rare plants from an uncertain future. However, some plants have proved difficult to produce through propagation. *Trillium*, for example, requires approximately seven years to grow from seed to flowering size. Wildflower brokers say that, at present, with wild plants so inexpensive and accessible, little financial incentive exists to start commercial propagation of *Trillium*.

In the Netherlands, propagation of the giant snowdrop (*Galanthus elwesii*) has also been difficult. This species is native to a part of the world where the winters are cold and the summers hot and dry. With the Dutch climate characterized by mild temperatures and frequent and plentiful rainfall, propagation of the giant snowdrop has not yet been a commercial success. Efforts are currently under way to improve propagation technology of *Galanthus elwesii* in the Netherlands; production was estimated at 100,000 bulbs in 1991. Still, that falls short of large-scale propagation. Dutch bulb brokers continue to rely on wild-collected giant snowdrop imports to supply the commercial demand. (Note: this species should not be confused with the most readily available snowdrop species, the common snowdrop [*Galanthus nivalis*] which in the vast majority of cases is propagated.)

The long time required for some species to reach salable size and the difficulty in propagation techniques are two of the most important factors that inhibit commercial propagation initiatives and make collection from the wild appealing. While propagation can be time-consuming and expensive, buying from local collectors is quick and inexpensive. Thus, a cheap and available labor force contributes to the continuation of the trade by offering bulbs and wildflowers at prices that allow industry a wide profit margin.

Not least importantly, trade in wild plants continues due to lack of awareness on the part of the consumer. Many of today's gardeners are unaware of conservation concerns and do not know which species are rare, threatened, or endangered. Nor do many know whether their plants are of wild or propagated origin. Information about plant origins has recently appeared in some catalogs, but is not featured in the vast majority and has only just begun to appear on packaging labels. When asked, many brokers are unable to answer questions about the origins of the plants they sell.

II.

Wild Plant Collection in Perspective

The plight of wild plants has received substantial publicity in recent years. Newspapers, magazines, books, and even television shows have featured the issue of collection from the wild, more often than not wholly condemning the practice because of the depletion of genetic variability in wild plant populations, the possibility of extinction in the wild, and the degradation of the landscape.

The bulb industry of the Netherlands produces approximately 8.5 billion bulbs per year, while importing about 50 million wild bulbs, primarily from Turkey. World trade in orchids totaled about 9.3 million plants in 1989; over 10 percent were likely to be of wild origin. Cacti, also popular among plant collectors and southwestern gardeners, are predominantly grown in nurseries; yet approximately 15 percent of the 7.5 million cacti recorded in international trade in 1989 were collected from the wild. Thus, although the great collecting days of the past are gone, a substantial number of wild-collected plant species continue to appear in trade.

While some of these plants are collected by professionals hired and sent out by the horticultural industry, many others are gathered by the people who live in rural areas. From the Appalachian mountains where generations of families have earned extra income from the collection of native wildflowers and herbs, to the hills of Turkey where peasants go out each spring to harvest many of our favorite bulbs, local people may depend on revenue derived from plant collection to feed and clothe their families.

Profits from wild plants supplement meager incomes in these regions, which typically contain subsistence-level agricultural communities with few if any other opportunities for local employment. Most collectors are not paid much for the plants they collect. In Turkey, wholesale prices per bulb vary by species and by age of the plant; *Cyclamen*'s value is around U.S.$150 per 1,000 and snowdrops around U.S.$32 per 1,000. The Venus flytrap (*Dionaea muscipula*), an insectivorous plant native to several counties in North Carolina and South Carolina, is also collected from the wild. Collectors have reported receiving as little as $0.07 per plant. A Venus flytrap may retail for $5.00. Depending on the species, commercial exporters and importers make enormous profits from the collection and sale of wild plants. At the same time, local harvesters also earn basic revenue that they cannot afford to ignore. If these people are denied access to a valued resource, such as the native flora, they may lose their appreciation for it — and, insofar as possible, may convert the land to a more profit-yielding use.

Unfortunately, many plant species collected from the wild have become rare in the wild. People are trying to earn income from plant populations that are decreasing rapidly. In this case, both man and nature lose.

The Harvest: How Much Is Too Much?

The problem, in a word, is overexploitation. Resource utilization is a reality throughout the world, and, with utilization, there is always the possibility of overexploitation. A rate of harvest that causes a species to diminish more rapidly than it can reproduce is known as an unsustainable harvest.

The American alligator became endangered in the 1960s due to excessive hunting for its valuable skin. In response, federal and state governments began to protect the species by prohibiting any harvest and by implementing plans to conserve alligator habitat and encourage a favorable breeding environment. As a direct result of these efforts, the American alligator has recovered remarkably, and a limited harvest is now allowed in some states. Earnings from the sale of alligator hides now justifies the protection of many wetland areas inhabited by alligators.

Since the American alligator is a very conspicuous species, its disappearance from its native swamps became obvious quite rapidly. With plant populations, many of which are distributed over large areas and occur only sporadically, it is less evident when utilization is having an adverse impact on a species. How does one determine if a harvest rate is sustainable? How many individuals can be continuously removed from a population without causing the population to become depleted? What evidence leads to the conclusion that a species is being overexploited?

These are difficult questions. Evaluation of harvesting systems requires scientific data such as a species' population size, its reproductive strategies and rates, and the impact of removing individuals from the population. Following baseline studies of the status of the species in the wild, if harvesting takes place, monitoring is necessary to make sure that populations are not being depleted.

The vast majority of plants currently collected from the wild are harvested without any management plan or monitoring system. Harvest rates are rarely based on any sort of scientific information. Numerous plant populations, particularly of rare species, have been harvested unsustainably. Populations of the winter daffodil (*Sternbergia candida*), a rare bulb endemic to Turkey and first described as a new species in 1979, were rapidly reduced when commercial collectors harvested thousands at a time for the specialist market. This species may now be completely extirpated from its few known localities. The Minnesota trout lily (*Erythronium propullans*), another species popular among specialist collectors, has been overexploited to the extent that it was given protection under the U.S. Endangered Species Act in 1986.

Response to Uncontrolled Collection and Trade

Regulations affecting the collection of wild plants exist at state, national, and international levels. The government of Turkey, for example, has banned the export of certain bulbous species and has established export quotas for others. Mexico has gone even further and prohibited the export of any native plants or animals harvested from the wild.

The United States, through its Endangered Species Act, affords protection to plants, both native and foreign, that are listed under the act. Plants are classified as "endangered," meaning that a species is in danger of extinction throughout all or a significant portion of its range, or as "threatened," meaning that the species is likely to become endangered within the foreseeable future throughout all or a significant portion of its range. The Endangered Species Act protects species listed as endangered by

- prohibiting their import into or export from the United States;
- prohibiting interstate transport in them; and
- prohibiting their sale in interstate commerce.

Individual states also list species they consider endangered or threatened. Tennessee, for example, recently included the pink ladyslipper (*Cypripedium acaule*) on its list of endangered plants. This listing prohibits collection from the wild.

The Convention on International Trade in Endangered Species of Wild Fauna and Flora (CITES) promotes conservation by allowing trade in wildlife that can tolerate certain levels of collection and by prohibiting trade in species that are threatened with extinction. CITES offers three categories of protection, with species listed on one of three appendices that stipulate different levels of regulation.

An Appendix I listing, which is the most restrictive, pertains to species that are endangered by trade. The black rhino, the chimpanzee, and the giant panda, as well as *Paphiopedilum*, tropical Asian slipper orchids that are closely related to the North American ladyslippers, are listed on Appendix I of CITES. This listing prohibits any commercial trade involving wild species, or any part or derivative of these species, such as horn from rhino. Some trade is permitted under special circumstances, usually limited to educational and display purposes and scientific research. Trade in Appendix I species requires an export permit from the country of origin or a re-export certificate from the re-exporting country, as well as an import permit from the country destined to receive the wildlife.

An Appendix II listing allows trade in species that can withstand certain levels of exploitation but requires a monitoring and regulation system to record levels of trade. An Appendix II listing allows trade in both wild and propagated/captive-bred specimens. Wild specimens may be traded with an export permit from the country of origin or a re-export certificate from the re-exporting country. However, export permits are to be issued only if the specimens are legally acquired and if trade in the specimens is determined not to be detrimental to the survival of the species. Propagated plants may be traded with a certificate of artificial propagation. Among the plant species listed in Appendix II are the snowdrops (*Galanthus*), the winter daffodils (*Sternbergia*), *Cyclamen*, Venus flytrap (*Dionaea muscipula*), and ginseng (*Panax quinquefolius*).

Appendix III contains species subject to regulation within individual countries and for which the cooperation of other countries is sought to control that trade. Therefore, Appendix III is specific to exports of certain taxa from given countries.

As of November 1992, 117 countries were parties to CITES. With trade in wildlife monitored and regulated through a system of import and export permits, volumes of trade are recorded, and reports are submitted annually to the administering body of CITES, the CITES Secretariat, located in Lausanne, Switzerland. Enforcement of the treaty is the responsibility of each country; however, the Secretariat may assist individual governments in implementing the treaty.

CITES does not prohibit trade in plants or animals that are not endangered. Rather, the treaty is based on the theory that responsible resource utilization is a means to achieve conservation. When wildlife is not valued, it is not protected. CITES presumes that, by permitting trade in certain species that can withstand some harvest, those species are appreciated and regarded as worth conserving. Unfortunately, while this presumption works for some species, for others it may not.

Wild Plants and Gardens

Some gardeners believe that, by planting a rare species in their garden, they are contributing to the conservation of that species. Unfortunately, this usually is not the case. Plants existing in a garden are isolated from the gene pool; their genes do not contribute to the evolutionary process that allows species to survive in a world requiring genetic diversity to meet ecological challenges. There are a few cases — in particular, that of the Franklin tree (*Franklinia alatamaha*) — in which a species that has ceased to exist in its original habitat continues to be known and grown by horticulturists in many parts of the world. In such instances, however, the gene pool is far less diverse than it would have been in naturally occurring populations.

Some of our most coveted garden favorites — our hybrid daffodils, tulips, and lilies — owe their beauty and elegance to their wild relatives. Centuries of horticulturists have selected plants with valued qualities such as resistance to disease, hardiness, brilliance of color, and longevity. In designing a garden, today's gardener has a vast array of colors, sizes, and shapes from which to choose. This variety can be attributed to the endless efforts of plant breeders and to the wealth of genetic resources that make horticultural creations possible.

We should not underestimate the extent to which horticultural experimentation relies on the genes of wild plants. Reduction of plant populations and elimination of species, either through overcollection or loss of habitat, diminishes the options open to the plant breeders of future generations. One cannot foresee which blights and pests will be prevalent in the coming decades, nor what tints and patterns will be in vogue. By purchasing wild plants that may be rare or in decline, we may be contributing to the reduction of the floral gene pool. Because of our shortsighted actions, future horticulturists may be deprived of the tools to create the coming generations' disease-resistant garden treasures.

Moreover, climates where gardens are established may prove unsuitable to a wild species. For example, the rare Chilean crocus (*Tecophilaea cyanocrocus*) was collected from the wild for a botanical garden located in the Pacific Northwest. The plants thrived for many years but were wiped out during record low temperatures one winter. This scenario undoubtedly occurs frequently when bulbs are planted in unsuitable climates.

There are other problems, too. The pink ladyslipper (*Cypripedium acaule*), one of North America's most beautiful native orchids, is not propagated on a commercial scale. Rather, virtually all pink ladyslippers advertised for sale have been collected from the wild. This species is often thought of as being endangered; in fact, it occurs in significant numbers across a wide section of North America. The pink ladyslipper is collected for both horticultural and medicinal purposes. As an herbal remedy, its root is used to relieve headaches, insomnia, and various nervous disorders. As an addition to woodland and rock gardens, it is a delicate, delightful orchid that gardeners find particularly difficult, and often impossible, to grow. To survive, the pink ladyslipper must be planted in soil that contains a special fungus associated with the orchid's roots. Without this fungus, the orchid cannot absorb nutrients from the soil. As a result, most transplanted ladyslippers die after one year. It is for this reason that consumers should avoid purchasing the pink ladyslipper; it is senseless to purchase a plant that has no chance of survival.

III.

The Gardener's Role

Because of the lack of monitoring systems and management plans, consumers usually cannot be certain that the plants they want to buy are harvested sustainably. One strategy to promote conservation is to avoid buying individual plants of any species that is collected in the wild, unless sound scientific evidence indicates that the species is not being overcollected or unless the consumer is shown solid proof that an individual plant is propagated. By refusing to buy species whose status is unclear, gardeners can promote propagation as well as appropriate harvesting methods.

Exercising caution does not mean that gardeners have to sacrifice beauty in their gardens. Horticulturists in Europe and North America are producing hybrids and cultivars that are not only strong and free of disease but hardy and conditioned to survive in North American temperate gardens.

Because propagated plants are by and large young, strong, and healthy, they are also more reliable garden choices. With wild plants, a consumer may be buying an aged specimen or a plant with specific growing requirements that often are impossible to replicate. The consumer might also be purchasing a plant that has endured several hard years or rigorous transport conditions and therefore is in a weakened state. Many of the most exquisite wild bulbs, such as some miniature *Narcissus* species from Portugal and Spain, are small and unable to withstand long periods of storage and transport. During the journey from field to warehouse, then to truck or ship, and so on, before finally arriving at the garden, these bulbs can become desiccated and may even die. Moreover, gardeners may not realize the importance of planting such bulbs immediately. If smaller species bulbs are not planted until late fall, as are other bulbs, the interval is likely to result in few bulbs surviving to bloom in the spring.

Consumer Tips

Gardeners who are concerned about over-exploitation of wild plant populations can use their influence to send a message to plant distributors and retailers. Here are some ways to do that and to purchase wisely:

1. Before buying a plant, look for information about source.

    a. Check for *labels* on bulbs imported from the Netherlands. Are the labels in accordance with the terms of the labeling scheme described in chapter 4? Do bulbs sold loose in bins bear appropriate labels indicating source?

    b. Examine catalogs and advertisements for information about source. Do catalogs display a *disclaimer* or general statement about plant origins in the front of the catalog?

2. Critically evaluate the information about plant origins.

    a. Question ambiguous phrases, such as "nursery grown." Look for precise descriptions of propagation methods or claims of propagation so that there is no question whether plants are indeed propagated, that they have not been wild-dug and transplanted to a nursery setting. Obviously, plants of the latter type should be considered to be of wild origin despite their brief visit to the nursery.

b. Consider *price* as an indicator. Inexpensiveness may indicate that plants are of wild origin. Keep in mind, however, that propagated plants are usually of higher quality than wild-collected specimens.

3. If there is any ambiguity, question the vendor.

   a. Many plant vendors are brokers, rather than growers. For example, garden centers may purchase plants instead of growing them themselves. When asking a vendor about plant source, try to determine whether he or she is knowledgeable about the plants being sold.

   b. Ask the vendor about the method of propagation used for the particular species in which you are interested. Has it been propagated by division, from cuttings, or by seed? What length of time was required to go from seed or cutting to salable size? Is the length of time reflected in the price of the plant?

4. Consider growing plants from seed rather than purchasing plants of uncertain origin.

   a. A viable alternative is to grow many different plants from seed. Seed is available from various native plant societies, botanical organizations, and seed exchanges. Consultation with these groups is a useful way to increase your knowledge of propagation and cultivation and also a way to share information about plant conservation issues.

   b. You may wish to collect seed from wild plants. However, if you decide to follow this option, ethical collecting practices should be followed. For example, seed should be collected in small quantities, with sufficient seed always left to repopulate natural populations.

5. Voice your concerns.

   It is extremely important to speak up and explain your point of view. Often you can bring about changes because economics and reputation come into play, rather than genuine concern for plant conservation. If vendors understand your reluctance to purchase plants of dubious origin, they may make more of an effort to document the source of their plants.

6. Be aware of state and federal legislation protecting plants.

   a. Information about laws pertaining to plants is available from your state's natural resources department, and data concerning the conservation status of plants are available from the state Natural Heritage Program, or their equivalents. Contact the relevant agency in your state to learn about local conservation concerns and plant protection regulations.

   b. Report illegal activites to the appropriate agency, such as your state fish and game department.

7. When in doubt, contact plant societies, botanical gardens, and other conservation organizations to determine which nurseries or vendors sell propagated plants.

   Many organizations distribute lists of reputable nurseries. Be careful, however; the situation is ever-changing. Nurseries listed could begin to sell wild plants, or qualifying new nurseries or old nurseries with new policies could be excluded mistakenly. The best option is to consult on a regular basis with knowledgeable sources to determine where to buy your plants — and, always, keep asking questions until you receive satisfactory answers. (See "Sources of Information" following Part II.)

IV.

Making a Difference

A gardener may feel that his or her individual plant purchases, over the long run, do not make much difference in the great scheme of things. If the plant purchases of all the gardeners in the United States were totaled, however, the quantity would be quite significant. U.S. consumers purchase an estimated one billion bulbs annually; for wildflowers the number is unknown.

Ten years ago, few gardeners or plant suppliers were even remotely aware of the origin of their plants. But slowly, through the efforts of a few concerned individuals and later several conservation organizations and gardening and plant societies, the issue of wild-collection has become more widely discussed and acted on, and this has had a measurable impact. Publicity about the plight of wild plants, as well as campaigns to avoid purchases of wild-collected plants, have caused the industry to recognize plant conservation as a serious matter.

The Dutch Bulb Industry

Much of the progress that has been made in recent years has been with the bulb industry in the Netherlands. Initially, Dutch industry representatives were hesitant to disclose information about the origins of the species bulbs they sold, causing frustration among consumers earnestly seeking accurate data. Without definitive source data, concerned consumers felt it necessary to avoid buying species bulbs where it was known that collection from the wild was occurring. Public awareness campaigns encouraged the Dutch bulb industry to investigate the origins of some of their "Dutch" bulbs, many of which were in fact wild-collected in distant lands.

Additional pressure by conservation groups (World Wildlife Fund, the Natural Resources Defense Council, Garden Club of America, and the Fauna and Flora Preservation Society, which is based in the United Kingdom) led to an agreement to require accurate labels for bulbs from the Netherlands indicating whether the plants are propagated or of wild origin. As stipulated by this agreement:

- After July 1, 1990, all bulbs of specified species that are produced in and/or exported from the Netherlands were to be labeled "bulbs from wild source," if indeed they were of wild origin. The bulbs covered at this stage of the agreement consisted of species primarily collected from the wild, although some are propagated as well. For example, while about 10 million specimens of *Anemone blanda* were wild-collected in Turkey in 1990, approximately 19 million were propagated in the Netherlands. The specified species are

Anemone blanda
Arisaema spp.
Cardiocrinum giganteum
Cyclamen (except *Cyclamen persicum*)
Cypripedium spp.
Dracunculus spp.
Eranthis cilicicus
E. hyemalis
I. siberica ssp. elegantissima
I. kopetdaghensis
I. paradoxa
I. persica
I. tuberosa
Leucojum aestivum
L. vernum
Narcissus asturiensis

Galanthus (except *Galanthus nivalis*)
Iris acutiloba
N. bulbocodium ssp. conspicuus
N. bulbocodium ssp. tenuifolium
N. cyclamineus
N. juncifolius
N. rupicola
N. scaberulus
N. triandrus albus
N. triandrus concolor
Pancratium maritimum
Sternbergia spp.
Trillium spp.
Urginea maritima
Uvularia spp.

- After July 1, 1992, all species bulbs were to be labeled. Because mandatory labeling at this stage of the agreement is restricted to species bulbs, hybrid tulips and daffodils and other large hybrid bulbs are exempted.
- By 1995, all bulbs are to be labeled, including species bulbs, hybrids, and cultivars.

Labels, according to this agreement, must bear one of two phrases: "Bulbs from wild source" or "Grown from cultivated stock." The agreement is now statutory under Dutch law, so all bulb exports from the Netherlands are required to be labeled according to the agreement's terms. Brokers in other European countries and in the United States, however, have not yet signed this agreement and, thus, are not obligated to comply with its labeling requirements. Consequently, there are still numerous inconsistencies in the system that may confuse the consumer. Efforts are under way to encourage brokers outside the Netherlands to sign the agreement.

By 1995, then, consumers can expect to find labels, at a minimum, on all bulbs of Dutch origin. This is an important development for gardeners that will help to remove much of the ambiguity about source that has surrounded bulb shopping in the past. It is extremely important for consumers to keep up the pressure, so that other countries and institutions will follow the Dutch example.

Indigenous Propagation Projects

Many bulb and wildflower growers deal in plants that are native to other parts of the world. The number of commercial operations existing in countries where the plant species are native is quite small. Projects involving species of animals, such as farming of Nile crocodiles in southern Africa or raising tropical fish in Thailand for the aquarium trade, are far more developed than initiatives concerning plants. Nevertheless, this situation is beginning to change.

Prompted by environmental groups calling for conservation efforts at the source, propagation initiatives are now under way in Turkey. As part of the "Indigenous Propagation Project," sponsored by Dutch and Turkish traders and WWF and designed and implemented by the Bulb Research Centre (Lisse, the Netherlands), the Ataturk Central Horticultural Institute (Yalova, Turkey), the Fauna and Flora Preservation Society, and the Turkish Society for the Protection of Nature, experts from the United Kingdom and the Netherlands will work with Turkish scientists, bulb brokers, and local residents to establish propagation programs in rural areas. Local people will participate by tending bulb fields. In this way, they will continue to earn income from Turkey's floral resources, although the revenue will derive from propagation rather than collection. British conservationists and Dutch horticulturists are collaborating with Turkish botanists to determine the most promising species to plant, as well as the most successful strategies to use in growing the bulbs.

This project, while still at an early stage of development, is a giant step forward for bulb and wildflower conservation. By encouraging propagation of bulbs in native habitat, pressure will be taken off wild plant populations, local people will have a more reliable and continuing source of income, and consumers in Europe and North America will be able to expect a higher quality bulb. At present, British, Dutch, and Turkish horticulturists have selected several popular species for propagation, in particular the giant snowdrop (*Galanthus elwesii*) and Neapolitan cyclamen (*Cyclamen hederifolium*). Other species include *Sternbergia* spp., *Fritillaria* spp., *Eranthis* spp., Greek anemone (*Anemone blanda*),

Cyclamen cilicium, and *Cyclamen coum*. It will take several years before propagated bulbs become available for export, but once these bulbs are ready to be sold, consumers should make every effort to support this important endeavor.

World Wildlife Fund is committed to this kind of effort and to extending it to other parts of the world, including North America, so that more of the economic benefits of wild plant conservation are secured by the people who most need them.

Part II

Introduction

The remaining chapters of this guide are devoted to a species-by-species analysis which the gardener can refer to when visiting a garden center or when making selections from a catalog, to see whether plants are endangered or threatened or whether they are likely to be wild-collected or propagated.

Each of the following four chapters contains lists of temperate-zone plant species readily available to the U.S. gardener. The left-hand column consists of the species names as they are commonly advertised; as a result, some of the names are taxonomically incorrect. For this book to be useful for both botanists as well as gardeners, erroneous names are either corrected or explained in the "Notes" column.

The central column provides the reader with an idea whether the species in question is propagated or wild-collected. An attempt has been made to place plant species in one of two categories, either "W" for wild-collected, or "P" for propagated. Those having a "W" are species for which virtually all available plants are likely to have been collected from the wild. Some specialist horticulturists may be able to propagate these species, but propagated plants are not at present offered on a commercial scale. Plants characterized by a "P" are not collected from the wild for sale in commercial markets. Not surprisingly, many plant species are both wild-collected and propagated and are labeled "W, P."

Although this guide's intent is to provide the gardener with some definite information about wildflowers, bulbs, and other flowering garden plants available for purchase, conclusive evidence about the source of many of these plants remains elusive. The column devoted to "Notes" attempts to clarify some of the ambiguities by quantifying production of plants or levels of harvest from the wild. Information about the geographic origin of each plant species, as well as data pertaining to the conservation of the species, is also included in this section.

The conservation status information has been gleaned from numerous sources. Within the United States, state Natural Heritage Programs have been consulted to determine which native species are protected, which occur on state rare plant lists, and which have been given a ranking by The Nature Conservancy. The terminology used for the status descriptions for the various species varies enormously, with plants appearing on state rare plant lists as "Endangered," "Threatened," "Rare," "Special Concern," "Of Concern," "Sensitive," and so on. Unfortunately, definitions of these terms differ from state to state. The only consistent status ranks are those of the U.S. Endangered Species Act and The Nature Conservancy (TNC). According to TNC, "Critically Imperiled" means that the species is extremely rare, with 5 or fewer occurrences in the state; "Imperiled" means that the species is very rare, with between 6 and 20 occurrences in the state; "Rare" indicates that there are between 20 and 100 occurrences in the state.

International conservation status categories have also been noted, when they exist. The World Conservation Union (also known as the International Union for Conservation of Nature and Natural Resources, or IUCN) has standard terms for conservation ranks: "Extinct," "Endangered," "Vulnerable," "Not Threatened," and "Indeterminate." These terms are defined in the glossary at the back of the book. Listings in the Appendices of the

Convention on International Trade in Endangered Species of Wild Fauna and Flora (CITES; see p. 16) are also indicated.

When a species is protected by state law, it is so indicated. To find out what sort of protection is afforded the species, the reader should contact the individual state's Department of Natural Resources' Natural Heritage Program, or its equivalent.

Finally, circumstances are constantly changing. Many small nurseries may be developing propagation techniques to grow plants that are listed in this guide as originating exclusively from wild sources. Similarly, plants designated as propagated may be supplied by only a few nurseries that might conceivably go out of business. As an additional cautionary note, gardeners should be aware that while countries may ban the export of a particular species, this does not necessarily mean that plants of this species are not exported in contravention of national law. For consumers to have the most accurate information about their purchases, they must question vendors and perhaps investigate even further to get the most up-to-date information about source.

V.

North American Wildflowers

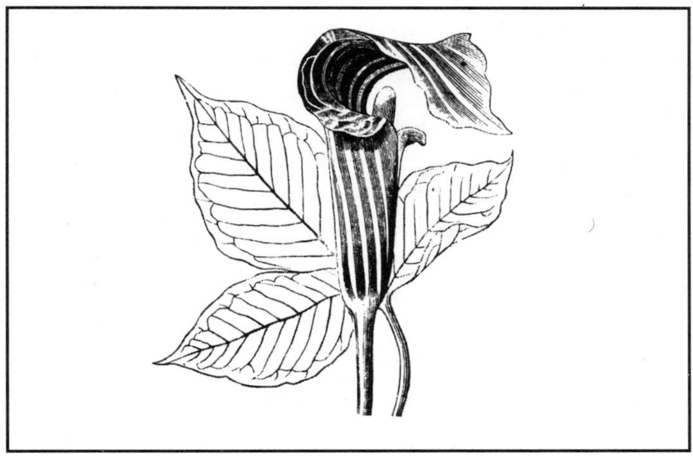

Black-eyed Susan, dragonroot, spring beauty, Dutchman's breeches, thimbleweed, and queen-of-the-prairie: the names of native wildflowers evoke memories and visions of our American heritage, the wild and natural areas that the colonists discovered when they first arrived, and the forests and grasslands that harbor these treasures today. Children play in swamps and woodlands amid the flamboyant cardinal flower and the proud and colorful irises. Roadsides throughout the nation support rich clumps of asters, coneflowers, and daisies, their colors made more incredible by their sheer numbers.

Wildflowers have long been appreciated and even revered. Gardeners and herbalists in particular have observed, enjoyed, cultivated, nurtured, and in many cases harvested native plants. In recent years, an increasing interest in nature and the environment has led to an upsurge in curiosity about native wildflowers, and gardeners with varying specialties and degrees of horticultural talent are trying their hand at cultivating them.

As interest grows, the number of gardeners seeking plants has also increased, forcing the market to accommodate demand by supplying larger quantities. Although many of these native plants are propagated in local nurseries, many, too, are collected from natural areas. Surprisingly, information about propagation is scanty or nonexistent. This lack of detailed knowledge means that gardeners are often unable to determine the origin of the plants they want to buy.

Some native plants are extremely common. Regardless of the ease of propagation, these plants are collected because they are readily available. Competition with vendors of wild-collected plants who offer stock at much-reduced rates presents a real problem for nurseries.

The reader will note the absence of some North American wildflowers from this chapter. Numerous bulbs are discussed in the bulb chapter. Many of these genera have distributions beyond North America; it seemed logical to put all the species occuring in the same genus together in one place. Similarly, North American terrestrial orchids are addressed in the orchid chapter. Insectivorous plants have also been given their own chapter.

North American Wildflowers

Genus, Species	Category	Notes
Acorus calamus (sweet flag; flagroot)	W, P	Northern Hemisphere; southern and eastern Asia, introduced into Europe through Turkey around 1550. Both wild-collected and propagated in the United States. Easily propagated by division.
Actaea pachypoda (white cohosh; white baneberry)	W, P	Eastern North America. Wild-collected and propagated in the United States. Propagation from seed or division; three years required to grow from seed to flowering size. Delaware: Critically Imperiled. Florida: protected and listed as Threatened; Critically Imperiled. Kansas: Critically Imperiled.

		Louisiana: Imperiled. Oklahoma: Critically Imperiled.
A. rubra (red baneberry)	W, P	North America. Wild-collected and propagated in the United States. Propagation from seed or division; three years required to grow from seed to flowering size. Indiana: protected and listed as Threatened. Kansas: Critically Imperiled. Ohio: protected and listed as Threatened.
Allium spp.	See chapter on Bulbs.	
Amsonia tabernaemontana (bluestar; blue dogbane)	W, P	Southeastern United States; also occurs from Massachusetts south to Delaware as an escaped species. Primarily propagated; some wild-collection occurs. Propagation by seed, cuttings or division. Kansas: Critically Imperiled. Tennessee: *A. tabernaemontana* var. *gattingeri* is listed as Special Concern. Virginia: Rare (TNC).
Anaphalis margaritacea (pearly ever-lasting)	P	North America, eastern Asia. Propagated by seed in the UnitedStates. Maryland: Rare. Virginia: Rare (TNC).
Anemone spp.	See chapter on Bulbs.	
Antennaria dioica (everlasting)	P	(Syn. *A. tomentosa.*) Northern North America, northern Asia, Europe. Propagated in United States.
A. tomentosa	See *A. dioica*.	
Aquilegia caerulea (columbine)	P	Rocky Mountains. Propagated in the United States. Easy to propagate from seed.

A. canadensis (wild columbine)	P	North America. Propagated in the United States. Propagation is relatively easy; two years required to go from seed to flowering size. Alabama: *A. canadensis* var. *australis* is listed as Critically Imperiled. Delaware: Critically Imperiled. Florida: *A. canadensis* var. *australis* is protected and listed as Endangered.
Aralia racemosa (American spikenard)	W, P	North America south to northern Mexico. Wild-collected and propagated from seed in the United States. Alabama: Critically Imperiled. Colorado: Rare. Delaware: Imperiled. Kansas: Critically Imperiled. Mississippi: Critically Imperiled. South Dakota: Rare.
Arisaema spp.	See chapter on Bulbs.	
Aruncus dioicus (goatsbeard)	W, P	North America and Eurasia, Belgium to Albania. Wild-collected and propagated in the United States. Propagation is slow by seed but rapid by division. Oklahoma: Critically Imperiled.
Asarum spp.	See chapter on Bulbs.	
Asclepias tuberosa (butterfly weed)	W, P	North America. Primarily propagated; some wild-collection. Maine: Endangered. New Hampshire: protected and listed as Endangered. Vermont: protected and listed as Threatened.
Aster laevis (aster)	P	North America. Propagated in the United States. Delaware: Critically Imperiled. Oklahoma: Critically Imperiled. New Mexico: Rare.
A. linariifolius (flax-leaved aster)	P	North America. Propagated in the United States. Numerous cultivars available. Iowa: protected and listed as Endangered. Kansas: Critically Imperiled.

A. novae-angliae (new england aster)	P	North America. Propagated in the United States. Oklahoma: Critically Imperiled.
Baptisia australis (wild false indigo; blue false indigo)	W, P	Pennsylvania south to North Carolina and Tennessee. Primarily propagated; some wild-collection. Propagation by seed, cuttings or division. Indiana: protected and listed as Endangered. Iowa: Special Concern. Maryland: protected and listed as Threatened. Ohio: protected and listed as Endangered.
B. leucantha (prairie false indigo)	W, P	Minnesota south to Mississippi and Texas. Primarily propagated; some wild-collection. Propagation by seed or division.
Brodiaea californica (California brodiaea)	P	California, Oregon. Propagated by seed or from offsets in the United States. Oregon: Threatened.
Calochortus spp. (mariposa lily)	W, P	North America from British Columbia and the Dakotas south to Guatemala. Primarily propagated; some wild-collection. Propagated by seed. Numerous species are protected in various states.
Caltha palustris (marsh marigold)	W, P	Eurasia, North America. Wild-collected and propagated in the United States. Propagation slow by seed, but reasonable by division. Delaware: Critically Imperiled. Kentucky: Endangered. Missouri: Endangered. Tennessee: protected and listed as Endangered.
Campanula rotundifolia (bluebell; harebell)	W, P	Northern Hemisphere. Wild-collected and propagated in the United States. Majority of plants available are of propagated origin. Maryland: Rare. Missouri: Endangered. Ohio: protected and listed as Threatened. West Virginia: Imperiled.

Caulophyllum thalictroides (blue cohosh)	W, P	New Brunswick south to Missouri and South Carolina. Wild-collected and propagated in the United States. Most plants of wild origin. Delaware: Imperiled. Kansas: Critically Imperiled. South Carolina: Of Concern; Imperiled. South Dakota: Rare.
Chelone lyonii (turtlehead)	W, P	North Carolina, South Carolina, Tennessee. Wild-collected and propagated in the United States. Propagation by seed or division; propagation by cuttings is easy and quick. Mississippi: Critically Imperiled.
Cimicifuga racemosa (black cohosh; false bugbane)	W, P	Ontario to Massachusetts, south to Georgia and Tennessee. Wild-collected and propagated in the United States. Propagation by seed or division. Illinois: protected and listed as Endangered. Massachusetts: protected and listed as Endangered. Mississippi: Imperiled.
Claytonia caroliniana (Carolina spring beauty)	W, P	Eastern North America. Wild-collected and propagated in the United States. Most plants collected from the wild. Alabama: Critically Imperiled. Minnesota: Special Concern. Ohio: Potentially Endangered.
C. virginica (Hammond's yellow spring beauty)	W, P	Eastern North America. Primarily wild-collected; some propagation in the United States. Easily propagated by division. Massachusetts: protected and listed as Threatened. New Jersey: *C. virginica* var. *hammondiae* is listed as Endangered and Critically Imperiled.
Clematis virginiana (leather flower)	W, P	North America. Wild-collected and propagated by seed and from cuttings in the United States. Oklahoma: Critically Imperiled.
Clintonia borealis (Clinton lily; corn lily)	W, P	Eastern North America. Wild-collected and propagated in the United States.

		Slow and difficult to propagate; majority of plants on sale are wild-collected. Indiana: protected and listed as Endangered. Maryland: protected and listed as Threatened. Ohio: protected and listed as Endangered. Tennessee: Special Concern.
C. umbellulata (speckled wood lily)	W, P	New Jersey and New York, south to Georgia. Primarily wild-collected; propagated in very small quantities by specialist growers in the United States. Ohio: protected and listed as Threatened.
C. uniflora (bride's bonnet)	W, P	British Columbia to central California. Primarily wild-collected; some propagation in the United States. Propagation by division is slow.
Coptis groenlandica (cankerroot)	W	Northeastern North America. Wild-collected in the United States. All propagation methods have proved extremely slow, although division of clumps is possible. West Virginia: Imperiled.
Coreopsis auriculata (tickseed; lobed tickseed)	P	Virginia south to Florida and Mississippi. Propagated in the United States. Several cultivars available. Mississippi: Imperiled.
C. grandiflora (tickseed)	P	Central and southern United States. Propagated in the United States.
C. lanceolata (lanceleaf tickseed)	P	Michigan to Florida and New Mexico. Propagated in the United States. Kansas: Imperiled.
C. verticillata (tickseed)	P	Maryland to Florida, west to Arkansas. Propagated in the United States. West Virginia: Imperiled.
Cornus canadensis (bunchberry)	W, P	Greenland, Labrador, andAlaska, south to New Mexico and West Virginia; also

		in eastern Asia. Wild-collected and propagated in the United States. Propagated from cuttings; more slowly by seed or division. Illinois: protected and listed as Endangered. Indiana: protected and listed as Endangered. Iowa: protected and listed as Endangered. Maryland: protected and listed as Endangered. New Jersey: Imperiled. Ohio: protected and listed as Threatened. Virginia: Critically Imperiled.
Dicentra canadensis (squirrel corn)	W, P	Quebec and Nova Scotia, south to North Carolina and Missouri. Wild-collected and propagated in the United States. Connecticut: Threatened. Maine: Threatened. Minnesota: Special Concern. New Hampshire: protected and listed as Threatened. New Jersey: Endangered; Critically Imperiled.
D. chrysantha (golden-eardrops)	W, P	Southern California and Baja California. Primarily wild-collected; some propagation by seed in the United States.
D. cucullaria (Dutchman's breeches)	W, P	Nova Scotia south to North Carolina and west to Kansas. Wild-collected; some propagation in the United States. Alabama: Imperiled. Delaware: Imperiled. Oklahoma: Critically Imperiled. Mississippi: Critically Imperiled. New Hampshire: protected and listed as Special Concern. South Carolina: Of Concern; Critically Imperiled.
Diphylleia cymosa (umbrella leaf)	W, P	Virginia south to Georgia and Tennessee. Primarily wild-collected; some propagation in the United States. Propagation from seed is easy but slow. Alabama: Critically Imperiled. South Carolina: Of Concern; Critically Imperiled. Virginia: Imperiled.

Dodecatheon meadia (shootingstar)	W, P	Pennsylvania west to Wisconsin and south to Alabama and Texas. Wild-collected and propagated in the United States. Propagation from seed is easy but slow; requires three years to bloom. Florida: protected and listed as Endangered; Critically Imperiled. Louisiana: Imperiled. Michigan: protected and listed as Threatened. Minnesota: Special Concern. Mississippi: Imperiled. Pennsylvania: protected and listed as Endangered. New York: Possibly Extirpated.
Echinacea pallida (purple coneflower)	W, P	Midwestern United States south to Louisiana, Alabama, and Georgia. Wild-collected and propagated by seed and root cuttings in the United States. Alabama: Imperiled. Tennessee: Threatened. Wisconsin: protected and listed as Threatened.
E. purpurea (eastern purple coneflower)	W, P	Ohio to Iowa, south to Georgia and Louisiana. Wild-collected and propagated by seed and root cuttings in the United States. Numerous cultivars available. Alabama: Imperiled. Florida: Critically Imperiled. Kansas: Critically Imperiled. Louisiana: Critically Imperiled.
E. tennesseensis (Tennessee coneflower)	W, P	North America. Wild-collected and and propagated in the United States. Species is listed as Endangered under the U.S. Endangered Species Act; known from only five populations. Tennessee: protected and listed as Endangered.
Erysimum menziesii (Menzies' wallflower)	P	North America. Propagated in the United States. Easily propagated by seed. California: protected and listed as Endangered.

Erythronium spp.	See chapter on Bulbs.	
Eupatorium coelestinum (mist flower; blue boneset)	P	New Jersey to Kansas, south to Texas, Florida, and the West Indies. Propagated by seed, cuttings and division in the United States. Delaware: Imperiled. New Jersey: Rare (TNC).
E. purpureum (Joe-Pye weed; thoroughwort)	W, P	Eastern North America. Primarily propagated; some wild-collection. Propagation by seed, cuttings and division. Louisiana: Critically Imperiled.
Filipendula rubra (queen-of-the-prairie)	P	Pennsylvania to Michigan, Iowa south to Georgia. Propagated by seed and division in the United States. Illinois: protected and listed as Threatened. Iowa: protected and listed as Endangered. Maryland: protected and listed as Endangered. Michigan: protected and listed as Threatened. Missouri: Endangered. Virginia: Imperiled.
Fritillaria spp.	See chapter on Bulbs.	
Gaillardia aristata (blanket flower)	P	Southwestern Canada to Oregon, east to North Dakota and Colorado. Propagated by seed and division in the United States.
Galax urceolata (wand flower)	W, P	Virginia to Georgia. Primarily wild-collected; some propagation in the United States. Propagation very slow from seed and division.
Gaultheria procumbens (wintergreen; teaberry)	W, P	Southern Canada to Georgia and Alabama. Primarily wild-collected; some nurseries propagate by division and cuttings. Illinois: protected and listed as Endangered. South Carolina: Of Concern; Critically Imperiled.
Gentiana affinis (Rocky Mountain pleated gentian)	W, P	British Columbia to California and the Rocky Mountains. Wild-collected and propagated in the United States.

		Minnesota: Special Concern. South Dakota: Rare.
G. alba (yellow gentian; pale gentian)	P	(Syn. *G. flavida.*) Northeastern North America. Propagated from seed in the United States. Indiana: protected and listed as Threatened. Kansas: Critically Imperiled. Kentucky: Endangered. Michigan: protected and listed as Endangered. Ohio: protected and listed as Endangered. Oklahoma: Critically Imperiled. Pennsylvania: Rare (TNC). Wisconsin: protected and listed as Threatened.
G. andrewsii (fringe tip closed gentian)	W, P	Eastern North America. Wild-collected and propagated in the United States. Propagation by seed is slow but easy. Delaware: Critically Imperiled. Maryland: protected and listed as Threatened. Massachusetts: protected and listed as Threatened. Missouri: *G. andrewsii* var. *andreswsii* is listed as Endangered. New Hampshire: protected and listed as Threatened. Vermont: protected and listed as Threatened. Virginia: Critically Imperiled.
G. austromontana (Appalachian gentian)	P	North America. Propagated in the United States. Tennessee: Threatened. Virginia: Imperiled.
G. bisetaea (gentian)	P	Southwestern Oregon. Propagated from seed in the United States.
G. calycosa (gentian)	P	British Columbia to California and the Rocky Mountains. Propagated from seed in the United States.
G. clausa (closed gentian)	W, P	Eastern North America. Often confused with *G. andrewsii*. Wild-collected and propagated by seed and division in the United States. Ohio: Potentially Threatened.

G. decora (gentian; showy gentian)	W, P	North America. Wild-collected and propagated in the United States. Kentucky: Threatened. Virginia: Rare (TNC).
G. flavida	See *Gentiana alba.*	
G. newberryi (Newbery's gentian; alpine gentian)	P	Mountains of California, Oregon, and western Nevada. Propagated from seed in the United States. Oregon: Threatened.
G. saponaria (soapwort gentian)	W, P	Pennsylvania to Illinois, south to Alabama and Louisiana. Wild-collected and propagated in the United States. Alabama: Rare (TNC). Delaware: Imperiled. Ohio: protected and listed as Endangered. Oklahoma: Critically Imperiled. Michigan: protected; Probably Extirpated. New Jersey: Rare (TNC). New York: protected and listed as Rare; Critically Imperiled.
G. villosa (Sampson's snakeroot striped gentian)	W, P	Eastern United States south of New Jersey. Wild-collected and propagated in the United States. Alabama: Critically Imperiled. Indiana: Extirpated. Maryland: protected and listed as Endangered. Ohio: protected and listed as Endangered. Pennsylvania: Rare (TNC). New Jersey: Probably Extirpated.
Geranium maculatum (wild geranium; wild crane's bill)	W, P	North America. Wild-collected and propagated in the United States. Seed propagation is easy; two years required to reach salable size. Louisiana: Critically Imperiled. South Dakota: Rare.
Gillenia trifoliata (Indian-physic; Bowman's root)	W, P	New York, Ontario, and Michigan, Michigan, south to Georgia and Alabama. Wild-collected and propagated by seed in the United States. Michigan: protected and listed as Threatened. Missouri: Extirpated.

Hedyotis caerulea (bluets)	W, P	(Syn. *Houstonia caerulea.*) Eastern North America. Wild-collected and propagated in the United States.
Helenium autumnale (common sneezeweed)	P	North America. Propagated in the United States. Numerous cultivars available.
Helianthus angustifolius (swamp sunflower)	P	New York south to Florida, west to Missouri and Texas. Propagated in the United States. Delaware: Imperiled. Illinois: protected and listed as Threatened. Missouri: Extirpated. New York: protected and listed as Threatened; Imperiled.
H. occidentalis (McDowell's sunflower)	P	North America. Propagated in the United States. Maryland: protected and listed as Threatened. Ohio: Potentially Threatened. Virginia: Critically Imperiled.
Heliopsis helianthoides (oxeye)	P	New York to Michigan, south to Georgia. Propagated in the United States. Several cultivars available. Delaware: Critically Imperiled.
Hepatica acutiloba (liverleaf)	W, P	Eastern North America. Wild-collected and propagated by seed and division in the United States. Three years required to go from seed to flowering size.
H. americana (liverleaf)	W, P	(Syn. *H. triloba.*) Eastern North America. Wild-collected and propagated in the United States. Three years required to go from seed to flowering size.
H. triloba	See *H. americana.*	
Heuchera maxima (alumroot)	W, P	Islands off southern California. California. Propagated by seed; wild-collection rare.

H. sanguinea (coralbells)	W, P	New Mexico and Arizona into Mexico. Wild-collected and propagated in the United States. Many cultivars are widely available.
Houstonia caerulea	See *Hedyotis caerulea.*	
Hydrastis canadensis (goldenseal)	W, P	Eastern North America. Wild-collected and propagated in the United States. Also collected extensively as a medicinal herb. Alabama: Imperiled. Connecticut: Endangered. Delaware: Rare (TNC). Georgia: protected and listed as Endangered. Maryland: protected and listed as Threatened. Massachusetts: protected and listed as Endangered. Michigan: protected and listed as Threatened. Minnesota: protected and listed as Endangered. Mississippi: Critically Imperiled. New York: protected and listed as Threatened; Imperiled. North Carolina: protected and listed as Endangered. Pennsylvania: protected and listed as Vulnerable. Tennessee: Threatened. Vermont: protected and listed as Endangered. Virginia: Rare (TNC).
Hypoxis hirsuta (star grass; yellow star grass)	W, P	Maine to Florida and Texas. Wild-collected and propagated from seed or division in the United States. Colorado: Presumed Extirpated. Delaware: Imperiled. Maine: Possibly Extirpated. New Hampshire: protected and listed as Threatened.
Iris spp.	See chapter on Bulbs.	
Jeffersonia diphylla (twinleaf)	W, P	Ontario to Iowa and south to Alabama. Wild-collected and propagated in the United States. Easily propagated from seed but slow to gain salable size. Alabama: Imperiled. Georgia: protected and listed as Endangered. Iowa: protected and listed as Endangered. Michigan:

		Special Concern. Minnesota: protected and listed as Threatened. New Jersey: Endangered; Critically Imperiled. New York: protected and listed as Rare.
Krigia montana (dwarf dandelion)	W, P	North Carolina to Tennessee and Georgia. Wild-collected and propagated in the United States. Tennessee: Threatened. Virginia: Critically Imperiled.
Lewisia brachycalyx (lewisia)	W, P	Southwestern United States. Wild-collected and propagated in the United States; also propagated in the United Kingdom.
L. columbiana (Columbia lewisia)	W, P	British Columbia to Oregon and California. Wild-collected and propagated from seed and division in the United States. Oregon: Threatened; *L. columbiana* var. *columbiana* is listed as Threatened; *L. columbiana* var. *wallowensis* is listed as Of Concern. Montana: Sensitive; Critically Imperiled.
L. columbiana var. *rupicola* (rosy lewisia)	W, P	Washington and Oregon. Wild-collected and propagated from seed and division in the United States. Oregon: Threatened.
L. cotyledon	W, P	Oregon and California. Wild-collected and propagated from seed and division in the United States. Now considered to be Rare (IUCN); listed in Appendix II of CITES. Oregon: *L. cotyledon* var. *howellii* is listed as Of Concern; *L. cotyledon* var. *purdyi* is listed as Threatened.
L. nevadensis	W, P	Washington to California, east to Rocky Mountains. Wild-collected and propagated from seed and division in the United States.

L. oppositifolia (opposite-leaved lewisia)	W, P	Northern California and southern Oregon. Wild-collected and propagated from seed and division in the United States. Oregon: Of Concern.
L. rediviva (bitter root)	W, P	British Columbia to northern California, east to Rocky Mountains. Wild-collected and propagated from seed and division in the United States.
L. tweedyi	W, P	British Columbia and Washington. Wild-collected and propagated from seed and division in the United States. Now considered to be Rare (IUCN); listed in Appendix II of CITES.
Liatris aspera (blazing-star)	W, P	Ontario and South Dakota, to South Carolina and Texas. Primarily wild-collected; some propagation from seed, division, and offsets. Virginia: Critically Imperiled.
L. pycnostachya (cattail gay-feather)	W, P	North America. Wild-collected and propagated from seed and division in the United States. Indiana: protected and listed as Endangered.
L. spicata (spiked blazing-star)	W, P	Eastern New York, south to Florida. Primarily propagated; some wild-collected. Propagation from seed and division. Delaware: Critically Imperiled. Maryland: Highly Rare. Missouri: Extirpated.
Lilium spp.	See chapter on Bulbs.	
Linnaea borealis (twinflower)	W, P	North America, northern Europe to the Carpathian and Ural Mountains. Wild-collected and propagated from seed, division and cuttings in the United States. Difficult to establish in warmer climates. Connecticut: *L. borealis* var. *americana* listed as Special Concern and Extirpated. Indiana: Extirpated. Iowa: protected and listed as Endangered.

		Maryland: protected and listed as Endangered; Possibly Extirpated. New Jersey: Endangered. Ohio: Presumed Extirpated.
Lobelia cardinalis (cardinal flower)	W, P	New Brunswick to Minnesota, south to Florida and Texas. Primarily propagated; some wild-collected. Several cultivars available.
L. elongata (elongated lobelia)	P	Propagated in the United States. Delaware: Critically Imperiled.
L. siphilitica (blue cardinal flower)	W, P	Maine to South Dakota, south to Mississippi. Primarily propagated; some wild-collected. Maine: Possibly Extirpated. Massachusetts: protected and listed as Threatened.
Maianthemum canadense (two-leaved Solomon's seal; wild lily-of-the-valley)	W, P	South Dakota to Georgia and Tennessee. Wild-collected and propagated in the United States. Very easy to propagate from division. Kentucky: Threatened.
Marshallia grandiflora (large-flowered Barbara's-buttons)	W, P	Pennsylvania to North Carolina and Tennessee. Wild-collected and propa gated in the United States. Kentucky: Endangered. Maryland: protected and listed as Endangered; Possibly Extirpated. Pennsylvania: protected and listed as Endangered. Tennessee: protected and listed as Endangered. West Viriginia: Imperiled.
Mertensia virginica (Virginia bluebells)	W, P	New York to Alabama, west to Kansas. Wild-collected and propagated in the United States. Propagation easy but slow from seed. Delaware: Rare (TNC). Michigan: protected and listed as Threatened. Mississippi: Critically Imperiled.

Mimulus ringens (Allegheny monkey flower)	W, P	Nova Scotia west to Manitoba, south to Virginia and Texas. Wild-collected and propagated in the United States. Idaho: Critically Imperiled. Louisiana: Imperiled. Mississippi: Imperiled.
Mitchella repens (Partridge berry)	W, P	Eastern and central North America. Wild-collected and propagated from seed, cuttings and division in the United States. Iowa: protected and listed as Endangered. Oklahoma: Imperiled.
Mitella diphylla (coolwort)	W, P	Eastern North America. Wild-collected and propagated in the United States. Propagation from seed and division easy but slow. Delaware: Imperiled.
Monarda didyma (beebalm; Oswego tea)	P	New England south to Georgia and Tennessee. Propagated in the United States. Easily propagated by division. Many cultivars available. Michigan: protected and Possibly Extirpated. New Jersey: Imperiled.
M. fistulosa (horsemint)	P	Eastern North America. Propagated in the United States. Easily propagated by division. Delaware: Critically Imperiled. New York: *M. fistulosa* var. *clinopodia* is protected and listed as Rare. West Viriginia: *M. fistulosa* var. *brevis* is listed as Imperiled.
Oenothera missouriensis (evening primrose)	W, P	Missouri and Kansas to Texas. Primarily propagated; some wild-collection. Tennessee: protected and listed as Endangered.
O. tetragona (evening primrose)	W, P	Eastern United States. Propagated in the United States. Primarily propagated; some wild-collected.
Pachysandra procumbens (Allegheny spurge)	W, P	Kentucky to Florida and Louisiana. Wild-collected and propagated from division and cuttings in the United States. Alabama: Rare (TNC). Florida:

		protected and listed as Endangered; Critically Imperiled. Louisiana: Imperiled. Indiana: protected and listed as Endangered. Mississippi: Rare (TNC). South Carolina: Of Concern; Critically Imperiled.
Penstemon barbatus (beard-tongue)	P	Utah to Mexico. Propagated in the United States. Propagation primarily from seed; also from division. Several cultivars available.
P. digitalis (beard-tongue)	W, P	Maine to South Dakota, south to Texas. Propagated in the United States. Primarily propagated from seed and division; some wild-collected.
P. hirsutus (hairy beard-tongue)	W, P	Maine to Virginia and Wisconsin. Propagated in the United States. Primarily propagated; some wild-collected. Several cultivars available.
P. lemhiensis (beard-tongue)	P	Idaho. Propagated from seed and division in the United States. Montana and Idaho: Imperiled. Montana: Threatened.
P. smallii (beard-tongue)	W, P	North Carolina and Tennessee. Wild-collected and propagated by seed and division in the United States.
Phlox bifida (sand phlox)	W, P	Michigan to Kansas, Arkansas and Tennessee. Wild-collected and propagated in the United States. Easily propagated by seed and cuttings. Indiana: *P. bifida* ssp. *stellaria* (cleft phlox) is listed as Endangered. Iowa: protected and listed as Threatened. Kentucky: *P. bifida* ssp. *stellaria* is listed as Threatened. Michigan: protected and listed as Threatened. Missouri: *P. bifida* ssp. *stellaria* is listed as Rare. Tennessee: *P. bifida* ssp. *stellaria* is listed as Threatened.

P. divaricata (wild sweet William; woodland blue phlox)	W, P	Quebec to Michigan, south to Georgia and Alabama. Primarily propagated; some wild-collected. Easily propagated from cuttings. New Jersey: *P. divaricata* var. *divaricata* is listed as Endangered; Critically Imperiled. South Dakota: Presumed Extirpated.
Physostegia virginiana (obedience)	W, P	New Brunswick to Minnesota, south to Missouri and South Carolina. Primarily propagated; some wild-collected. Propagation by seed and division. Many cultivars are available. Vermont: protected and listed as Threatened.
Podophyllum peltatum (mayapple)	W, P	Quebec to Florida and Texas. Wild-collected and propagated in the United States; also propagated in the Netherlands. Easily propagated by seed and division. Florida: Critically Imperiled.
Polemonium reptans (Jacob's ladder; Greek valerian)	W, P	New Hampshire to Georgia, west to Oklahoma. Primarily propagated; some wild-collected. Easily propagated by seed, division, and cuttings. Delaware: Imperiled. Kansas: Imperiled. Michigan: protected and listed as Threatened. Mississippi: Critically Imperiled. New Jersey: Endangered; Critically Imperiled.
Polygonatum biflorum (Solomon's seal)	W, P	Eastern North America. Primarily wild-collected; some propagation. Propagation easy but slow from seed, moderately fast from division. Delaware: *P. biflorum* var. *commutatum* is listed as Critically Imperiled. Michigan: *P. biflorum* var. *melleum* is protected and listed as Possibly Extirpated. New Hampshire: *P. biflorum* var. *commutatum* is protected and listed as Endangered.

P. commutatum (great Solomon's seal)	W, P	New Hampshire to Manitoba, south to George and northern Mexico. Wild-collected and propagated in the United States. Propagation by seed is slow and not that easy; moderately fast from division.
Potentilla tridentata (three-toothed cinquefoil)	W, P	Greenland; Wisconsin south to Georgia. Wild-collected and propagated in the United States. Propagation by seed and division is relatively slow. Connecticut: Endangered. Georgia: protected and listed as Endangered. Iowa: protected and listed as Threatened. New Jersey: Endangered; Critically Imperiled. Tennessee: Special Concern.
Pycnanthemum montanum (mountain mint)	P	Eastern North America. Propagated in the United States. South Carolina: Of Concern; Critically Imperiled. Virginia: Rare: (TNC).
Rudbeckia fulgida (orange coneflower)	P	New Jersey to Illinois, south to Alabama. Propagated from seed, cuttings, and division in the United States. Delaware: *R. fulgida* var. *fulgida* is listed as Critically Imperiled. Indiana: *R. fulgida* var. *palustris* and *R. fulgida* var. *umbrosa* are Extirpated; *R. fulgida* var. *deamii* is protected and listed as Endangered; *R. fulgida* var. *fulgida* is protected and listed as Threatened. New Jersey: Endangered.
R. hirta (black-eyed Susan)	W, P	Maine to Illinois, south to Georgia. Primarily propagated; some wild-collection. Propagation from seed, cuttings, and division. Many cultivars available. New Jersey: Endangered.
Ruellia humilis (wild petunia)	P	Pennsylvania west to Nevada, south to Texas and northern Florida. Propagated from seed, cuttings, and division in the United States. Maryland: protected and

		listed as Endangered; Possibly Extirpated. Michigan: protected and listed as Threatened. Minnesota: protected and listed as Endangered. Pennsylvania: protected and listed as Endangered. Virginia: Rare (TNC). Wisconsin: protected and listed as Endangered.
Sanguinaria canadensis (bloodroot)	W, P	Eastern North America. Wild-collected and propagated in the United States. Propagation is easy but slow from seed, moderately fast from division. Also collected from the wild for medicinal purposes. Louisiana: Imperiled.
Sedum nevii (Nevius' stonecrop)	W, P	Alabama and Tennessee. Primarily propagated; some wild-collected. Alabama: Imperiled. Tennessee: protected and listed as Endangered.
Shortia galacifolia (oconee-bells)	W, P	Virginia to Georgia. Wild-collected and propagated in the United States. Propagated by division and runners. Now considered to be Rare (IUCN); listed in Appendix II of CITES. Georgia: protected and listed as Endangered. North Carolina: protected and listed as Endangered. South Carolina: Of Concern; Imperiled.
Silene virginica (fire pink)	W, P	New Jersey to Minnesota, south to Georgia and Oklahoma. Wild-collected and propagated in the United States. Propagation from seed, cuttings, and division. Kansas: Critically Imperiled. Louisiana: Critically Imperiled. Michigan: protected and listed as Threatened.
Silphium perfoliatum (cup plant)	W, P	Ontario and South Dakota to Georgia, Mississippi, and Oklahoma. Primarily propagated; some wild-collected. Michigan: protected and listed as Threatened.

Sisyrinchium campestre (blue-eyed grass)	W, P	Illinois to Manitoba, south to Louisiana and Texas. Wild-collected and propagated in the United States. Easily propagated by seed and division.
Smilacina racemosa (false spikenard; false Solomon's seal)	W, P	North America. Wild-collected and propagated in the United States. Propagation by seed and division is easy but slow. Louisiana: Critically Imperiled.
S. stellata (star flower)	W, P	North America. Wild-collected and propagated in the United States. Propagation by seed and division is easy but slow. Kentucky: Endangered. Maryland: protected and listed as Endangered. Tennessee: protected and listed as Endangered. West Virginia: Critically Imperiled.
Solidago nemoralis (goldenrod)	W, P	Eastern and central North America. Primarily propagated; some wild-collected.
Stachys tenuifolia (hedge nettle)	P	New York to Minnesota, south to Alabama and Texas. Propagated from seed and division in the United States. Connecticut: Special Concern; Extirpated. Maine: *S. tenuifolia* var. *hispida* is Possibly Extirpated. South Carolina: *S. tenuifolia* var. *latidens* is listed as Special Concern and Critically Imperiled.
Stokesia laevis (Stoke's aster)	P	South Carolina to Louisiana and Florida. Propagated from seed and division in the United States. Numerous cultivars available.
Stylophorum diphyllum (celandine poppy)	W, P	Eastern United States. Wild-collected and propagated in the United States. Easily propagated by seed. Alabama: Critically Imperiled.

Talinum spinescens (spinescent fameflower)	P	Washington. Propagated from seed in United States. Oregon: Threatened.
Thermopsis caroliniana (Carolina lupine)	W, P	North Carolina to Georgia. Wild-collected and propagated by seed and division in the United States.
Tiarella cordifolia (foamflower)	W, P	Nova Scotia to Georgia and Alabama. Wild-collected and propagated in the United States. Propagation by seed and division is easy but slow. Mississippi: Imperiled. New Jersey: Endangered; Critically Imperiled. Wisconsin: protected and listed as Endangered.
Tradescantia ohiensis (Ohio spiderwort)	W, P	New England to Minnesota, south to Florida and Texas. Wild-collected and propagated in the United States. Easy to propagate from seed, cuttings, and division. Minnesota: Special Concern. New York: protected and listed as Special Concern; Critically Imperiled.
T. virginiana (common spiderwort; Virginia spiderwort)	W, P	Connecticut to Georgia, west to Missouri. Wild-collected and propagated in the United States. Easily propagated by seed, cuttings, and division. Delaware: Critically Imperiled. Michigan: Special Concern.
Trillium spp.	See chapter on Bulbs.	
Triteleia bridgesii	W, P	Oregon and California. Wild-collected and propagated in the United States.
T. crocea (yellow brodiaea)	W, P	(Syn. *Brodiaea crocea.*) Oregon and California. Wild-collected and propagated in the United States. Oregon: Of Concern.
T. hyacinthina (wild hyacinth)	W, P	British Columbia to Idaho, California, and Nevada. Wild-collected and propagated in the United States. Propagated by meristem culture in the Netherlands.

T. ixioides (pretty-face)	W, P	Oregon, California. Wild-collected and propagated in the United States. Oregon: Threatened.
Trollius laxus (spreading globe-flower)	W, P	Eastern United States. Primarily propagated; some wild-collected. Propagation by seed and division. Connecticut: Endangered. New Jersey: *T. laxus* ssp. *laxus* is listed as Endangered and Critically Imperiled. New York: *T. laxus* ssp. *laxus* is protected and listed as Threatened. Ohio: protected and listed as Endangered. Oregon: *T. laxus* var. *albiflorus* is listed as Threatened. Pennsylvania: protected and listed as Endangered.
Uvularia grandiflora (large-flowered bellwort)	W, P	Quebec to Minnesota, south to Oklahoma and Tennessee. Primarily wild-collected; some propagation in the United States. Propagation slow from seed, rapid by division. Connecticut: Endangered. Kansas: Imperiled. Maryland: Highly Rare. New Hampshire: protected and listed as Endangered. Oklahoma: Imperiled. South Dakota: Rare.
U. perfoliata (strawbell; perfoliate bellwort)	W, P	Quebec to Ohio, south to northern Florida and Louisiana. Primarily wild-collected; some propagation. Propagation slow by seed, rapid by division. New Hampshire: protected and listed as Endangered.
Vernonia noveboracensis (ironweed)	W, P	Massachusetts to Mississippi. Primarily propagated; some wild-collected. Propagated by seed, cuttings and division. Kentucky: Endangered.
Veronicastrum virginicum (Culver's root)	W, P	Massachusetts to Manitoba, south to Florida and Texas. Primarily propagated; some wild-collected. Alabama: Imperiled. Massachusetts: protected and listed as Special Concern.

		South Dakota: Rare. Vermont: protected and listed as Endangered.
Viola canadensis (Canada violet)	W, P	New Brunswick south to Alabama and west to Rocky Mountains. Wild-collected and propagated in the United States. Easily propagated by seed. Alabama: Rare (TNC). Connecticut: Threatened. Illinois: protected and listed as Endangered. New Jersey: Endangered; Critically Imperiled. Oregon: *V. canadensis* var. *rugulosa* is listed as Threatened.
V. pedata (bird's-foot violet)	W, P	Eastern United States. Wild-collected and propagated in the United States. Propagated from seed and division; root cuttings produce plants in one year. Delaware: Critically Imperiled. New Hampshire: protected and listed as Threatened. Ohio: protected and listed as Threatened.
V. pubescens (downy yellow violet)	W, P	Nova Scotia to North Dakota, south to Mississippi and Georgia. Wild-collected and propagated in the United States. Easily propagated by seed. Louisiana: *V. pubescens* var. *eriocarpa* is listed as Critically Imperiled. Mississippi: *V. pubescens* var. *eriocarpa* is listed as Critically Imperiled.
Zizia aurea (golden alexanders)	P	New Brunswick to Florida and Texas. Propagated in the United States. Delaware: Critically Imperiled.

VI.

Bulbs

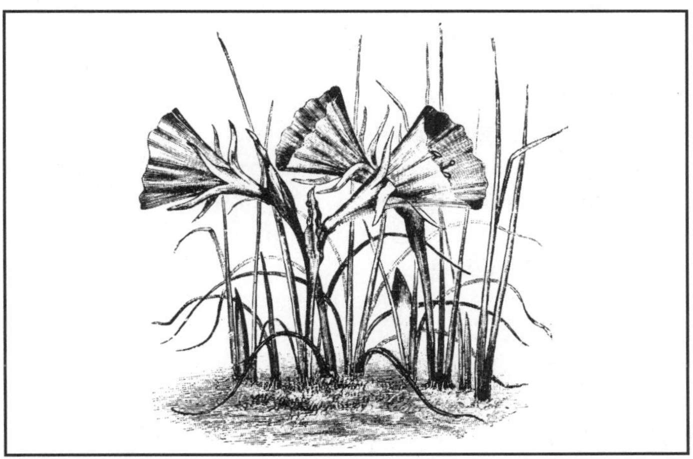

The most commonly traded bulb genera available to the temperate zone gardener in the United States occur within seven plant families: Ranunculaceae, Araceae, Aristolochiaceae, Iridaceae, Amaryllidaceae, Primulaceae, and Liliaceae. Most of these species are considered "bulbs," which is a general term usually used for plants that store food and water for long periods of time in underground parts. Technically, bulbous plants have either true bulbs, tuberous roots, tuber-corms, corms, or rhizomes. Many plants with bulbs or bulb-like structures grow in particularly demanding climates. In the Mediterranean region, where many bulbs originate, the climate is typified by cool winters with rain or snow and hot and dry summers. During these periods, growth is greatly reduced and often impossible. Plants have only a limited time frame in the spring and fall to grow and reproduce. They make use of stored nutrients and water to survive periods of drought, heat, or cold.

While the forms of "bulbs" may differ, common qualities have led to their popularity within the horticultural community. Bulbs are fairly easily transported and stored due to their ability to withstand desiccation better than nonbulbous plants. They are relatively tough and can survive a certain amount of handling that would cause other plants to perish.

Once again, it cannot be overemphasized that popularity and widespread availability do not indicate that plants are of propagated origin. Many well-known garden flowers have been collected from the wild for decades and continue to be collected. In short, do not rely on preconceived notions — check this guide, and, if doubt remains, question the grower or vendor.

As noted previously, certain species that might otherwise be included in the North American wildflower chapter appear in this chapter instead. Several genera in particular, *Trillium, Erythronium, Iris, Lilium, Arisaema, Asarum,* and *Fritillaria* are well represented in North America. For reasons of simplicity, these genera have each been treated as a whole, rather than split between the two chapters.

ALLIUM

Allium, an enormous genus comprising over 700 species, contains several members that are extremely important food crops. Most alliums are inedible; some have an extraordinarily unpleasant odor. Yet onions, garlics, leeks, chives, and shallots are staples in cooking pots across the world. While allium is usually viewed as a vegetable garden plant, its blossom is quite extraordinary. Only a few alliums are widely cultivated as ornamentals, but those few offer unusually large and showy globose flower heads that are excellent selections for sunny gardens and also interesting additions to dried flower arrangements. The giant onion (*Allium giganteum*) is particularly noteworthy, with enormous purple inflorescenses perched atop two-foot-long stems.

Members of the *Allium* genus are quite easy to grow and often increase beyond control. An example is *A. triquetrum,* a native of Europe that is now considered an invasive species in the

United States. Some alliums, such as the common onion, are biennials, and others are perennials, such as the shallots. Many of the perennial alliums are known as multipliers because each bulb will divide over a summer and produce several more bulbs. Multipliers are particularly valued among fanciers of shallots and potato onions; they commonly increase by 12, and sometimes by as many as 30, bulbs each year. Although not all species of *Allium* are quite so prolific, propagation from offsets is regarded as the easiest and fastest method of producing alliums; the horticulturist can expect to produce a salable bulb from an offset within two to three years.

Propagation of alliums by seed requires some time commitment but is relatively simple. Seedlings can be planted out after two seasons, and for some species after just one season, although a period of four to five years is necessary to produce a bulb of salable size.

Because alliums increase so rapidly by offsets as well as by seed, they are, for the most part, propagated rather than wild-collected. Growers in the Netherlands produce such significant quantities of these plants that most of the alliums sold by Dutch dealers are grown in that country. Nevertheless, Dutch importers do buy some bulbs from brokers in France and Turkey, as well as the propagated *A. schubertii* from Israel. Sufficient collection of alliums still occurs for some countries to have taken measures to reduce the pressure of collection. Turkey, for example, has banned the export of wild-collected rosy onion (*A. roseum*), a species that is now being propagated in the Netherlands.

ALLIUM (Liliaceae)

Species	Category	Notes
A. aflatunense	P	Central China. Propagated in the Netherlands.
A. albopilosum	See *A. christophii.*	
A. ampeloprasum (wild leek; levant garlic)	P	Southern Europe, western Asia. Propagated in Israel and the United States.

A. atropurpureum	P	Bulgaria, Romania, western Turkey. Propagated in the Netherlands.
A. azureum	See *A. caeruleum.*	
A. bulgaricum	See *A. siculum.*	
A. caeruleum	P	(Syn. *A. azureum.*) Siberia (Russia). Propagated in the Netherlands.
A. cernuum (nodding onion; wild onion)	W, P	(Syn. *A. recurvatum.*) Allegheny Mountains of North America. Both propagated and wild-collected in the United States. Propagated in the Netherlands. Iowa: protected and listed as Threatened Minnesota: protected and listed as Threatened. New York: protected and listed as Rare; Imperiled.
A. christophii (star-of-Persia)	P	(Syn. *A. albopilosum.*) Turkestan; Asia Minor. Propagated in the Netherlands under both names: *A. albopilosum* and *A. christophii.* Classified as Endangered in Turkey (IUCN).
A. cowanii	P	Southern Europe, Asia Minor. Propagated in the Netherlands.
A. cyaneum	P	China. Uncommon in cultivation. Propagated in the United States. Propagated on a small scale in the Netherlands.
A. elatum	See *A. macleanii.*	
A. fistulosum (scallion; welsh onion)	P	Siberia (Russia). Cultivated extensively.
A. flavum (yellow onion)	P	Southern Europe. Propagated in the United States and the Netherlands.
A. giganteum (giant onion)	P	Central Asia. Propagated extensively in the Netherlands and the United States.

A. hirtifolium	P	Iran. Some propagation in the Netherlands.
A. karataviense	P	Central Asia. Extensively propagated in the Netherlands.
A. luteum	See *A. moly*.	
A. macleanii	P	(Syn. *A. elatum.*) Central Asia, Uzbekistan. Propagated in the Netherlands under name of *A. elatum*.
A. moly (golden garlic)	P	(Syn. *A. luteum.*) Eastern Spain and southwestern France. Propagated extensively in the Netherlands and the United States. Good for perennializing; will spread fairly rapidly.
A. multibulbosum	P	Mediterranean. Propagated in the Netherlands.
A. neapolitanum (daffodil garlic; Naples onion)	P	Northern Italy. Propagated in the Netherlands and the United States.
A. oreophilum	P	(Syn. *A. ostrowskianum.*) Central Asia. Propagated in the Netherlands and the United States; a cultivar, 'Zwanenburg', is available. Classified as Rare in Turkey (IUCN).
A. ostrowskianum	See *A. oreophilum*.	
A. pulchellum	P	(Syn. *A. carinatum* ssp. *pulchellum.*) Mediterranean. Propagated in the United States. Propagated in small quantities in the Netherlands.
A. ramosum	P	(Syn. *A. odorum* and *A. tartaricum.*) Central Asia. Propagated in the United States. Propagated in very small quantities in the Netherlands.
A. rosenbachianum	P	Northern Afghanistan. Propagated in very small quantities in the Netherlands.

A. roseum (rosy onion)	P	European Mediterranean Region. Propagated in the Netherlands. Previously wild-collected in Turkey; export of wild specimens is now banned. Classified as Vulnerable in Turkey (IUCN).
A. schoenoprasum (chives)	P	Northern Hemisphere. Readily raised from seed; easily divided. Colorado: Rare. Michigan: protected and listed as Threatened. Minnesota: *A. schoenoprasum* var. *sibiricum* is listed as Special Concern. New York: Critically Imperiled.
A. schubertii	P	Eastern Mediterranean. Propagated in small quantities in the Netherlands; also propagated in Israel and Japan.
A. senescens ssp. *senescens*	P	Europe to Siberia. Common in cultivation. Propagated in the United States.
A. siculum	W, P	Southern Europe. Both *A. siculum* and *A. bulgaricum* are now regarded as belonging in the genus *Nectaroscordum*. Some taxonomists recognize one species with two subspecies: *Nectaroscordum siculum* ssp. *siculum*, and *N. siculum* subsp. *bulgaricum*. Wild-collected in Turkey. Propagated in the Netherlands.
A. sphaerocephalon (ballhead onion)	W, P	(Syn. *A. descendens.*) United Kingdom, Europe north to Belgium and east to Russia and Iran. Propagated extensively in the Netherlands. Previously overcollected in the United Kingdom but now collection is restricted. Classified as Rare (IUCN) in the United Kingdom.
A. stipitatum	P	Turkestan, Afghanistan, Central Asia. Excellent for cut flowers. Propagated in the Netherlands.

A. tricoccum (wild leek)	?	North America. Delaware: Imperiled.
A. triquetrum	W, P	Europe; western Mediterranean. Wild-collected in Portugal. Propagated in small quantities in the Netherlands. Now naturalized in the United States and regarded as an invasive exotic weed.
A. tuberosum (garlic chive)	P	(Syn. *A. uliginosum.*) Widely grown in Far East as perennial cash crop. Propagated in the United States.
A. unifolium (one-leaved onion)	W, P	Oregon and California. Propagated in the Netherlands. Oregon: Of Concern.
A. ursinum ssp. *ursinum* (wild leek)	W, P	Europe and the Caucasus (Russia). Wild-collected in Hungary. Propagated in the Netherlands.
A. victorialis	W	Southern Europe, northern Asia, Aleutian Islands. Wild-collected in Japan. Protected by law in Hungary.

ANEMONE

Anemone, known as the windflower or lily of the field, is a large genus of over 120 species primarily occurring in the north temperate zone. Anemones have been favorites among gardeners and hybridizers for many years; species were cultivated in Europe as early as the 16th century. French and British horticulturists were especially intrigued by its delicate, simple blossoms. These enthusiasts developed numerous cultivars that were available on a commercial scale during the 1700s and 1800s. Although interest in rare cultivars waned in the 19th century, two popular cultivars of the poppy anemone (*A. coronaria*, 'de Caen' and 'St. Brigid') continue to delight gardeners with their colorful spring blooms.

Although anemones are well known and widely available in the United States, the actual number of species in trade here is relatively small. Most of these species are nonbulbous and cannot be traded as "bulbs." Those that have tuberous roots are sometimes traded; because they are vulnerable to desiccation, they are frequently coated with wax before shipment to avoid drying out.

Aside from the popular cultivars, the most heavily traded anemone is the Greek anemone (*A. blanda*). This species is propagated in the Netherlands in enormous quantities but is also collected from natural areas in Turkey. During the 1988-1989 commercial season, Dutch brokers imported over 10 million wild-collected anemones from Turkey. Production of *A. blanda* is increasing in the Netherlands, yet the endeavor is a lengthy process. Although anemones are easily propagated by seed, lifting, or dividing, it usually takes about seven years for a seed-grown plant to reach marketable size.

ANEMONE (Ranunculaceae)

Species	Category	Notes
A. atrocoerulea	P	Cultivar of *A. blanda*; should be listed as *A. blanda* cv. 'Atrocoerulea.'
A. blanda (Greek anemone)	W, P	Southeastern Europe and Turkey. Wild-collected in Turkey. Propagated by the millions in the Netherlands. Many cultivars available. Classified as Vulnerable in parts of its range (IUCN).
A. canadensis (Canada anemone)	W, P	North America. Wild-collected and propagated in the United States. Connecticut: Endangered. Maryland: protected and listed as Endangered; Extirpated. New Jersey: Presumed Extirpated. Tennessee: protected and listed as Endangered. West Virginia: Critically Imperiled.

A. caroliniana (Carolina anemone)	W	Eastern United States. Alabama: Imperiled. Indiana: Extirpated. Tennessee: protected and listed as Endangered. Wisconsin: protected and listed as Endangered.
A. coronaria (poppy anemone)	P	Southern Europe to Asia. Propagated in the Netherlands. Used in hybridization; many cultivars available, including 'de Caen' and 'St. Brigid.' Classified as Vulnerable in Turkey (IUCN).
A. japonica	P	Material under this name may be *A. hupehensis* var. *japonica*, but usually it is a hybrid: *A. hupehensis* var. *japonica* x *A. vitifolia*.
A. nemorosa (wood anemone)	P	Europe. Propagated in small quantities in the Netherlands. Popular cultivars are *A. nemorosa* cv. 'Alba Plena' and *A. nemorosa* cv. 'Allenii.' Protected in France.
A. praecox	—	No reference can be found for this listing.
A. pulsatilla (pasque flower)	P	United Kingdom to Ukraine. Propagated in the Netherlands. Cultivars include *A. pulsatilla* cv. 'Rubra.'
A. quinquefolia (wood anemone)	W, P	Quebec south to North Carolina, Ohio, and Kentucky. Wild-collected and propagated in the United States. Mississippi: Critically Imperiled. Missouri: Endangered. South Dakota: Rare.
A. ranunculoides	P	Europe to Asia. Long in cultivation. *A. ranunculoides* ssp. *ranunculoides* is classified as Rare in Turkey (IUCN).
A. sylvestris	P	Europe and Siberia. Stoloniferous. Propagated in the United States. Protected in France.

A. virginiana (thimbleweed; tall anemone)	W, P	Nova Scotia south to South Carolina and west to Kansas. Wild-collected and propagated in the United States. Easily propagated by seed or division. Louisiana: Critically Imperiled.
A. vitifolie	W, P	Northern India, western China. The cultivar *A. vitifolie* cv. 'Robustissima' is available.

ARISAEMA

Many naturalists and gardeners are familiar with the North American native Jack-in-the-pulpit, which is one of over 200 species in the genus *Arisaema*. This plant has long fascinated plant enthusiasts because of its curious bloom, called a spadix, which is actually a spike supporting many tiny flowers surrounded by a sheath. *Arisaema* is distributed throughout Asia and parts of tropical Africa and North America, although most species occur in Japan, China, and the Himalayas. Despite their strange inflorescences and lovely leaves, few species are in cultivation. Most species of *Arisaema* prefer shade, moisture, and cool temperatures. They can be propagated by seed and also by lifting and separating the tuberous roots, but commercial propagation remains limited. Some species have become threatened in their natural habitats because of overexploitation. The level of export of wild plants from Japan, in particular, has caused concern in conservation circles.

ARISAEMA (Araceae)

Species	Category	Notes
A. dracontium (green dragon; dragon root)	W, P	Maine south to Florida and west to northeastern Mexico. Connecticut: Special Concern. Delaware: Imperiled. Massachusetts: protected and listed as Threatened. New Hampshire: protected and listed as Endangered. Vermont: protected and listed as Endangered.

A. speciosum	W	Himalayas, China. Wild-collected in India.
A. tortuosum	W	Northern India. Wild-collected in India.
A. triphyllum (Jack-in-the-pulpit)	W, P	North America. Some propagation in the United States, but most plants are wild-collected.

ASARUM

Asarum, known as wild ginger, is a large genus of approximately 75 species that occurs primarily in Japan but is distributed throughout the north temperate zone. Most *Asarum* species are valued for their foliage and are planted as ground covers in woodland gardens. Shade, moisture, and rich soil are required for successful cultivation; the creeping rhizomes of *Asarum* do not tolerate dry conditions. Propagation of *Asarum* is by division and by seed.

ASARUM (Aristolochiaceae)

Species	Category	Notes
A. arifolium	W, P	Southeastern United States. Both propagated and wild-collected.
A. canadense (wild ginger)	W, P	Eastern North America. Both propagated and wild-collected. Easy to propagate by seed, division, and cuttings. Louisiana: Critically Imperiled. Maine: Threatened. Mississippi: Imperiled. South Dakota: Rare.
A. caudatum	W, P	British Columbia to California. Both propagated and wild-collected in the United States. Propagation by seed, division, and cuttings.

A. caulescens	—	No reference can be found for this listing.
A. europeaum	P	Europe. Propagated in the United States and the Netherlands.
A. hartwegii	W, P	Oregon and California. Both propagated and wild-collected. Propagation is easy but relatively slow.
A. shuttleworthii	W, P	Southeastern United States. Propagated in the United States.

CHIONODOXA

Chionodoxa — named "glory of the snow" for its blossoms that emerge in early spring while snow still blankets the ground — is a small genus containing nine species. Occurring in the mountainous regions of Turkey and Crete, it is quite hardy.

Species of *Chionodoxa* are easily cultivated and propagated. Plants produce numerous offsets that thrive in a variety of soil types, provided there is adequate moisture. Seed propagation is also practical as germination is readily achieved. The popularity of these bulbs, as well as their ease of propagation, has led growers in the Netherlands to produce billions of *Chionodoxa* bulbs per year. The species *Chionodoxa luciliae*, as well as several of its cultivars, is produced in enormous quantities. Even so, *C. luciliae* is still wild-collected in Turkey, as are *C. sardensis, C. siehei*, and *C. tmoli.*

Unfortunately, difficulties in determining correct taxonomy for this genus have caused some confusion with nomenclature. *Chionodoxa luciliae* and *C. siehei* seem especially difficult to separate, with *C. siehei* continually misnamed in trade as *C. luciliae*.

CHIONODOXA (Liliaceae)

Species	Category	Notes
C. luciliae	W, P	(Syn. *C. gigantea.*) Western Turkey. Wild-collected in Turkey. Propagated by the millions in the Netherlands. This

		species is different from "*C. luciliae* of gardens," also known as "Maw's Chionodoxa," which is actually *C. siehei*. *Chionodoxa siehei* often appears in trade under the name *C. luciliae*.
C. sardensis	W, P	Western Turkey. Wild-collected in Turkey. Propagated in the Netherlands.
C. siehei	W	Turkey. Frequently sold incorrectly as a vigorous form of *C. luciliae*. "*C. luciliae* of gardens" or "Maw's Chionodoxa" is *C. siehei*.
C. tmoli	W, P	Turkey. Considered by some authorities to be a form of *C. siehei*. Wild-collected in Turkey. Propagated in small quantities in the Netherlands.

COLCHICUM

The meadow saffron is often confused with plants in the genus *Crocus* and is even sometimes called the autumn crocus, despite its membership in the genus *Colchicum*. These two genera are similar in appearance, but gardeners can easily differentiate them by examining the flowers closely. While *Crocus* has three stamens, *Colchicum* has six. The foliage is different as well: the narrow leaves of *Crocus* are adorned with a thin white stripe, while *Colchicum* lacks stripes and the leaves are usually wider than those of *Crocus*.

Colchicum is a large genus of approximately 60 species, distributed from Britain across Europe and through the eastern Mediterranean to Iran and Turkestan. The common autumn crocus (*Colchicum autumnale*) has been important as a medicinal plant since the 1500s, when it was first used by the Arabs to treat gout. In later centuries, colchicums were more highly valued as ornamentals. Nevertheless, colchicine, which is derived from *C. autumnale*, is still used in modern medicine to cure gout, and by horticulturists in plant breeding.

The genus *Colchicum* contains three divisions: the fall-flowering group, which includes *C. autumnale, C. cilicicum,* and *C. speciosum*; the spring-flowering division, consisting of a single species, *C. luteum,* the only species with yellow blossoms; and those species that flower in early winter and have a crisscross pattern on their petals. Colchicums can be propagated by division or be raised from seed. After division, one can expect corms to flower in two to three years. Propagation by seed requires a greater time commitment; following germination, seedlings will be ready to plant out after four to five years. In general, the *C. luteum* is regarded as being more difficult to cultivate than the autumn-flowering species, which will increase rapidly if planted in a favorable location.

COLCHICUM (Liliaceae)

Species	Category	Notes
C. autumnale (common autumn crocus; meadow saffron)	P	(Syn. *C. autumnale* var. *minor*) Cultivated since the 16th century. Propagated in the Netherlands. Protected by law in Poland.
C. autumnale major	See *C. byzantinum.*	
C. byzantinum	P	(Syn. *C. autumnale* var. *major.*) Southeastern Europe. Cultivated since its introduction in 1629. This species appears not to produce seed; some say all produced now are propagated vegetatively. It is possible that this is a garden hybrid. Propagated in the Netherlands.
C. cilicicum	W, P	Southern Turkey. Wild-collected in Turkey. Propagated in small quantities in the Netherlands.
C. luteum	W, P	Northern India, Afghanistan, central Asia, southwest China. Wild-collected in India. Propagated in the Netherlands.

C. speciosum	W, P	Caucasus, Asia Minor. Turkey has set an export quota for this species of 50,000 wild bulbs per year. Propagated in small quantities in the Netherlands.
C. variegatum	W, P	Turkey, Aegean Islands. Wild-collected in Turkey. Propagated in the Netherlands.

CROCUS

The genus *Crocus* comprises approximately 100 species distributed throughout Europe and Central Asia. It is best known as the source of saffron, one of the most expensive culinary spices in the world. Used as flavoring and food coloring, one ounce of saffron is valued at $125 and consists of the stigmas of approximately 5,000 common saffron (*C. sativus*) blossoms. This species is cultivated widely in Europe, and especially in Spain, where the highest quality saffron is produced.

Crocus is also renowned as one of the most popular groups of bulbous plants. Most flower early in the spring, although some such as *C. sativus* bloom in autumn. The vast majority of crocuses available to the consumer are cultivars; few species bulbs are propagated to any great extent. A market does, however, exist for rare species, and growers in the Netherlands are experimenting to meet this demand.

By and large, crocuses are easy to grow. Propagation by seed is easily achieved, as the seeds germinate readily. While seed-grown plants will flower in approximately three to four years, the lifting of cormels is regarded as the most rapid method of propagation. In the Netherlands, approximately 500 hectares are under production with crocuses, primarily in cultivars.

Trade in wild specimens of *Crocus* is largely geared toward specialist collectors. In the past, crocuses were collected from the wild in Turkey. Now, however, export of wild *Crocus* is prohibited from Turkey. *Crocus* spp. are protected by law in Hungary.

CROCUS (Iridaceae)

Species	Category	Notes
C. ancyrensis	P	Central Asia. Propagated in the Netherlands on a large scale. In the past, this species was wild-collected and exported from Turkey. Export of wild specimens is now prohibited.
C. angustifolius (cloth of gold crocus)	P	(Syn. *C. susianus.*) Southwestern Russia, northeastern Turkey. A dwarf species known since 1597. Propagated in the Netherlands under the name *C. susianus.*
C. biflorus (Scotch crocus)	P	Southern and central Europe to Turkey. Widely grown in the 1700s in Europe; at present, numerous subspecies are propagated in the Netherlands.
C. cancellatus ssp. *cancellatus*	W, P	(Syn. *C. kotchyanus* and *C. cilicicus.*) Greece to Iran. Wild-collected in Turkey for use as a local food source; also sold in local markets in the region.
C. chrysanthus	W, P	(Syn. *C. croceus, C. annulatus* ssp. *chrysanthus*, and *C. skorpilii.*) Bulgaria to Turkey. Some wild-collection; collection is banned in Turkey. One of the most popular crocuses. Many cultivars are grown in the Netherlands in vast quantities. Over 104 hectares were planted in 1991 with *C. chrysanthus* cultivars. The majority of *C. chrysanthus* offered are cultivars and therefore of propagated origin.
C. cilicicus	See *C. cancellatus.*	

C. flavus ssp. *flavus*	W, P	(Syn. *C. aureus, C. lacteus, C. lagenaeflorus, C. luteus* and *C. maesiacus*.) Yugoslavia to Turkey. Wild-collected in Turkey (export now banned). Propagated in small quantities in the Netherlands. In cultivation for at least 400 yrs. The most popular common yellow crocus. The well-known 'Dutch Yellow,' which is believed to be a hybrid between *C. flavus* and *C. angustifolius*, is propagated in the Netherlands.
C. fleischeri	W, P	Eastern Aegean Islands and Turkey. Wild-collected in Turkey; export now banned. Propagated in small quantities in the Netherlands.
C. goulimyi	P	Southern Greece. Propagated in small quantities in the Netherlands. This species produces many offsets. Classified as Rare (IUCN) and protected by law in Greece.
C. grandiflorus	See *C. vernus* ssp. *vernus*.	
C. karduchorum	P	Southeastern Turkey, eastern Iraq, western Iran. Propagated in small quantities in the Netherlands.
C. kotschyanus ssp. *kotschyanus*	W, P	(Syn. *C. zonatus*.) South and central Turkey, northwest Syria, central and northern Lebanon. Collected as a food source by locals in Turkey. Propagated in small quantities in the Netherlands. This species is very popular and is easily propagated as it produces prolific offsets. There are several subspecies, some which have been introduced as recently as 1980.
C. medius	P	Southeastern France and northwestern Italy. Propagated in small quantities in the Netherlands.

C. napolitanus	See *C. vernus* ssp. *vernus*.	
C. ochroleucus	P	Eastern Mediterranean region. Propagated in the Netherlands.
C. pulchellus	P	Greece and Turkey. Long in cultivation; propagated in the Netherlands. Many cultivars available.
C. purpureus	See *C. vernus* ssp. *vernus*.	
C. sativus (saffron crocus)	P	Europe. Now widely cultivated in Europe, especially Spain.
C. sieberi	P	Greece and Crete. Several subspecies occur in Yugoslavia, Bulgaria, and Albania. Propagated in the Netherlands. The cultivar 'Violet Queen' is particularly popular.
C. speciosus	P	Southeastern Europe to Turkey. Numerous cultivars produced in the Netherlands. Widespread in the wild.
C. tommasinianus	P	Yugoslavia. Propagated in the Netherlands; numerous cultivars available. Seeds freely.
C. vernus ssp. *vernus* (Dutch Crocus)	W, P	(Syn. *C. napolitanus*.) Central and southern Europe. Also known as the "wild crocus of the Alps and Pyrenees." Has been cultivated for many years; now a wide selection of cultivars is available to the gardener.
C. zonatus	See *C. kotchyanus* ssp. *kotchyanus*.	

CYCLAMEN

The genus *Cyclamen* is best known for its hybrids and selections of *C. persicum*, which are ever-present in florist shops across the United States. With beautifully patterned foliage and large flowers ranging from shades of red and pink to white, *C. persicum* selections are the product of almost 200 years of plant breeding. Other *Cyclamen* have also long interested gardeners; of an estimated 20 species, most are in cultivation. Few of these species, however, are propagated commercially. Except for *C. persicum*, the vast majority of *Cyclamen* in trade are of wild origin.

In 1973, in response to growing concern over the quantity of *Cyclamen* appearing in trade and threats to species in the wild, *Cyclamen* became the first genus of bulbs to be protected under the Convention on International Trade in Endangered Species of Wild Fauna and Flora (CITES). The genus is listed on Appendix II of this international treaty, thereby requiring trade to be regulated by a system of permits and certificates. (For a general discussion of CITES, see chapter 2.) Enforcement has been difficult, specifically because the Netherlands did not accede to CITES until 1984 and Turkey, the source of many *Cyclamen* species, has yet to do so. In 1985, however, in response to the need for improved export documentation from Turkey, the European Community temporarily banned all imports of *Cyclamen* from Turkey. Later, the ban was replaced by a yearly import quota of one million wild-collected *Cyclamen* bulbs, but this was exceeded in both 1986 and 1987. By way of explanation, Turkish exporters claimed that exports included cultivated stock, which was not subject to the quota. In 1988, a team from the European Community went to Turkey to investigate. Their journey revealed that all of the *Cyclamen* exported as cultivated was, in fact, stock that had been transplanted from the wild.

National legislation in Turkey to protect native *Cyclamen* species was enacted in 1983 by Decree no. 83/7540 of the Council of the Ministry of Agriculture. This decree banned the export of five species: *C. mirabile, C. repandum, C. pseudibericum, C trochopteranthum*, and *C. parviflorum*. At present, *Cyclamen* is exported from Turkey under a quota system. In 1992, the quota for the genus was 1,750,000 wild bulbs to be filled with *C. hederifolium* (1,250,000), *C. coum* (150,000), and *C. cilicium* (350,000).

Although the gardener can be relatively certain that the *Cyclamen* (other than *C. persicum*) encountered in retail centers and in catalogs are collected from the wild, some small-scale propagation efforts are being carried out in the United States and the United Kingdom. Far more promising, however, are initiatives in Turkey to propagate *Cyclamen* from seed. Several commercial growers are already experimenting with Neapolitan cyclamen (*C. hederifolium*) and *C. cilicium*. The time period required to produce a flowering-size plant from seed varies among species. For *C. persicum* in cultivation, it can be as short as nine months, but for other hardy species it can be several years. Turkish growers expect their seed-grown plants to be available in 1994 if all goes according to plan.

CYCLAMEN (Primulaceae)

Species	Category	Notes
C. africanum	W, P	North Africa. Propagated in very small quantities in the United States by specialist growers. Listed in Appendix II of CITES.
C. balearicum	W, P	Southern France and the Balearic Islands. Propagated in very small quantities in the United States by specialist growers. Abundant in the wild. Listed in Appendix II of CITES.
C. cilicium	W, P	Turkey. Wild-collected in Turkey; export quota set at 350,000 wild bulbs per year. Some propagation from seed has begun in Turkey, but stock is not yet available. Propagated in very small quantities by specialist growers in the Netherlands and the United States. Classified as Vulnerable in Turkey (IUCN). Listed in Appendix II of CITES.
C. coum ssp. *coum*	W	Eastern Europe to Turkey, the Caucasus, Iran, Syria and Lebanon. Wild-collected in Turkey. Propagated in very small quantities by specialist growers in the Netherlands and the United States. Classified as Vulnerable (IUCN). Listed in Appendix II of CITES.

C. coum ssp. *caucasicum*	W, P	Turkey, Caucasus, Iran. Propagated in very small quantities by specialist growers in the United States. Listed in Appendix II of CITES.
C. creticum	W	Crete, Karpathos. Classified as Not Threatened in Greece (IUCN). Listed in Appendix II of CITES.
C. cyprium	W, P	Cyprus. Propagated in very small quantities by specialist growers in the United States. Classified as Not Threatened in Cyprus (IUCN). Listed in Appendix II of CITES.
C. europeum	See *C. purpurascens.*	
C. graecum	W, P	Greece, Turkey, eastern Mediterranean islands. Wild-collected in Turkey. Propagated in very small quantities by specialist growers in the United States. Classified as Vulnerable in Turkey (IUCN). Listed in Appendix II of CITES.
C. hederifolium (Neapolitan cyclamen)	W, P	(Syn. *C. neapolitanum.*) Mediterranean region from Italy to Turkey. Wild-collected in Turkey; export quota set at 1,250,000 wild bulbs per year. Export banned from Italy. *C. hederifolium* forma *album* is also wild-collected. In Turkey, artificial propagation is under way for *C. hederifolium* and *C. hederifolium* forma *album*. Propagated in very small quantities by specialist growers in the Netherlands and the United States. Classified as Vulnerable in Turkey (IUCN). Listed in Appendix II of CITES.
C. indicum	—	This name is a mystery to botanists. Originally named from a drawing rather than a specimen, the drawing does not represent any known species.

C. intaminatum	W, P	Turkey. Propagated in very small quantities by specialist growers in the United States. Listed in Appendix II of CITES.
C. libanoticum	W, P	Lebanon. Propagated in very small quantities by specialist growers in the United States. Listed in Appendix II of CITES.
C. mirabile	W, P	Southwestern Turkey. Export of wild plants from Turkey is prohibited, yet bulbs are still exported from Turkey. Propagated in very small quantities by specialist growers in the United States. Classified as Endangered. Listed in Appendix II of CITES.
C. neapolitanum	See *C. hederifolium.*	
C. parviflorum	W	Turkey. Export from Turkey is prohibited. Listed in Appendix II of CITES.
C. persicum (florists' cyclamen)	W, P	Eastern Mediterranean. Most of the *Cyclamen* sold in florist's shops are hybrids and selections of this species, and are propagated in the Netherlands. Also propagated in Israel, Canada and the United States. Wild-collected in Turkey. Classified as Vulnerable in Turkey (IUCN). Listed in Appendix II of CITES.
C. pseudibericum	W, P	Southern Turkey. Export from Turkey is prohibited. Propagated in very small quantities by specialist growers in the United States. Classified as Vulnerable (IUCN). Listed in Appendix II of CITES.
C. purpurascens ssp. *purpurescens*	W, P	(Syn. *C. purpurescens.*) Eastern France to Bulgaria, possibly in the Caucasus. Previously known as *C. europaeum;* that name, however, is confusing because it represents several species and has been

NEWFS: New England Wild Flower Society.

Viola pedata

Dorothy Long, NEWFS

Echinacea purpurea

Dorothy Long, NEWFS

Claytonia virginica

Dorothy Long, NEWFS

Sanguinaria canadensis

Lilium philadelphicum

George Lienau, NEWFS

Catherine Heffron, NEWFS

Lilium canadense

Nina Marshall

Narcissus cyclamineus

Nina Marshall

Crocus pulchellus

Eranthis hyemalis

Nina Marshall

Nina Marshall

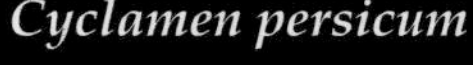

Cyclamen persicum

Nina Marshall

Tulipa greigii

Nina Marshall

Iris reticulata

Galanthus elwesii

Nina Marshall

Nina Marshall

Scilla sp.

Frank Bramley, NEWFS

Iris versicolor

NEWFS

Trillium grandiflorum

Fritillaria meleagris

Lucien Taylor, NEWFS

Carol Fyler, NEWFS

Erythronium americanum

Jean Baxter, NEWFS

Trillium undulatum

Judy Sellers, Garden Club of America

Colchicum sp.

Urgenia maritima

Judy Sellers, Garden Club of America

Nina Marshall

Sarracenia purpurea

WWF

Dionaea muscipula

Nina Marshall

Drosera sp.

Pleione formosana

Nina Marshall

Linda R. McMahan

Cypripedium calceolus var. *pubescens*

TRAFFIC USA

Cypripedium acaule

William Krebs

Cypripedium reginae

		rejected by taxonomists. Wild-collected in Hungary. Propagated in very small quantities by specialist growers in the United States. Protected by law in Czechoslovakia. Listed in Appendix II of CITES.
C. repandum ssp. *repandum*	W, P	Eastern Mediterranean and islands. Export from Turkey prohibited. Propagated in very small quantities by specialist growers in the United States. Classified as Indeterminate in Turkey (IUCN). Listed in Appendix II of CITES.
C. rohlfsianum	W	Libya. Classified as Vulnerable (IUCN). Listed in Appendix II of CITES.
C. trochopteranthum	W	Turkey. Export from Turkey is prohibited. Listed in Appendix II of CITES.

ERANTHIS

Most gardeners anxiously awaiting the arrival of spring are ultimately rewarded by the impatient blossoms of the scilla, the snowdrop, and the winter aconite, all renowned harbingers of the new season. The genus *Eranthis*, the winter aconite, consists of about seven species found in Europe and Asia. The two species most familiar to gardeners are *E. hyemalis* and *E. cilicicus*, both from southern Europe. Both species have been in cultivation for many years; *E. cilicicus* was first introduced in 1892.

In 1989, the government of Turkey set a quota of 10 million for wild-collected *E. hyemalis* bulbs. At present, some small-scale propagation efforts are under way in the Netherlands for both *E. hyemalis* and *E. cilicicus*, but production is still in the initial stages and is insignificant. Consequently, most *Eranthis* bulbs are of wild origin. If gardeners purchase *Eranthis* bulbs despite this fact, the bulbs should be planted immediately. Bulbs received by mail order in July cannot wait until September for planting; the bulbs are small and easily succumb to desiccation after a long period of storage and transport.

A hybrid between *E. cilicicus* and *E. hyemalis* propagated in the Netherlands is known as 'Guinea Gold' and is a better garden plant than either of the two species.

ERANTHIS (Ranunculaceae)

Species	Category	Notes
E. cilicicus	W, P	Greece, Turkey. Wild-collected in Turkey. Propagated in small quantities in the Netherlands.
E. hyemalis	W, P	Europe. Wild-collected in Turkey. Propagated in small quantities in the Netherlands. Classified as Vulnerable in Turkey (IUCN).

ERYTHRONIUM

Erythronium, commonly known as the dog-tooth violet or the trout lily, is a genus that has delighted Americans for centuries. Its approximately 25 species all occur in North America, except for *E. dens-canis* which is found in Europe and Asia. *Erythronium* species are spread across the United States, but most are native to the West Coast. Western species are generally larger, with more flowers and leaves that are more beautiful than are their eastern counterparts.

Erythronium is not considered difficult to grow, although it is not widely cultivated. All species prefer rich soil and moist, shady conditions. Bulbs tend to dry out rapidly once removed from the soil; hence, it is critical that they be planted immediately following purchase. Propagation is achieved most successfully through seed propagation. *Erythronium* sets seed freely and can reach flowering size within four years, although some species require five to six years.

The largest threat to *Erythronium* in the wild is undoubtedly loss of habitat. However, collection also threatens some populations. *Erythronium tuolumnense*, a species endemic to California, is considered to be threatened in the wild, and *E. propullans*, the Minnesota trout lily, is classified as endangered under the U.S. Endangered Species Act.

For the most part, *Erythronium* species in trade are wild-collected. Many of these species occur over wide ranges and in large numbers and are readily accessible to plant collectors. This situation, combined with the time commitment needed to produce a mature plant, perpetuates the trade in wild-collected specimens. Numerous American bulb and wildflower growers report no economic motivation to propagate *Erythronium*; collected easily, it is not financially worthwhile to propagate. Nevertheless, some propagation is under way. *Erythronium dens-canis* and *E. tuolumnense* are both propagated in the Netherlands, and *E. hendersonii* is propagated on a small scale. In addition, numerous delightful artificially propagated hybrids, including 'White Beauty' and 'Pagoda,' are widely available in the United States.

ERYTHRONIUM (Liliaceae)

Species	Category	Notes
E. albidum (white dog's-tooth violet; white trout lily)	W, P	East-central North America. Some propagation in the United States; most plants in trade are wild-collected. Alabama: Rare (TNC). Louisiana: Critically Imperiled. Maryland: protected and listed as Threatened. Mississippi: Critically Imperiled. Virginia: Imperiled.
E. americanum (yellow trout lily)	W, P	Eastern North America. Some propagation in the United States; most plants in trade are collected from the wild. Iowa: protected and listed as Threatened. Mississippi: Critically Imperiled.
E. californicum (fawn lily)	W	California.

E. citrinum	W, P	Oregon and California. Both propagated and wild-collected.
E. "*Citronella*"	P	Not a species; an artificial hybrid. Propagated.
E. dens-canis (dog-tooth violet)	W, P	Europe and Asia. Propagated in Europe by division. Propagated in the Netherlands; many cultivars available. Extinct in the wild in Turkey.
E. hendersonii	W, P	Oregon and California. Propagated in small quantities in the Netherlands and the United States.
E. japonicum	W, P	Japan. Some authorities believe this species to be *E. dens-canis* var. *japonicum*. Wild-collected in Japan. Propagated from seed in Japan, but not available in commercial quantities. Propagated in small quantities in the Netherlands.
E. klamathense	W, P	Oregon and California. Both propagated and wild-collected.
E. multiscapoideum	W	California.
E. oregonum	W, P	Southwestern Canada to Oregon. Both propagated and wild-collected.
E. "*Pagoda*"	P	Not a species; a popular hybrid between *E. revolutum* and *E. tuolumnense*. Excellent for perennializing.
E. revolutum (coast fawn lily)	W, P	Southwestern Canada to California. Both propagated and wild-collected. Oregon: Of Concern. Washington: Sensitive.
E. tuolumnense	W, P	Central California. Wild-collected in the United States. Propagated in the United States and the Netherlands. Classified as Indeterminate (IUCN).

E. umbilicatum	?	West Virginia and Virginia south to Alabama, western Georgia and northern Florida. Alabama: *E. umbilicatum* ssp. *umbilicatum* is listed as Critically Imperiled. Florida: protected and listed as Threatened; Imperiled.

FRITILLARIA

The genus *Fritillaria* contains approximately 85 species occurring in the Northern Hemisphere from North America through Europe and Asia to Japan. Species are concentrated in Turkey, which has 31 species, and Iran, which has around 20 species. North American species are considered to be some of the more fragile fritillaries and are less frequently found in cultivation.

Several species of *Fritillaria* are propagated extensively; others continue to be collected from the wild. Most gardeners are familiar with the stunning crown imperial, *F. imperialis,* whose orange or yellow blossoms stand atop stems that can reach as high as four feet. First cultivated in Europe in 1576, it has continued to impress gardeners with its sturdy long-lasting blooms. The crown imperial became so depleted by overcollection that its rarity prompted horticulturists to cultivate it on a commercial scale; it is now propagated in the Netherlands and also in Turkey. Export of all species of wild-collected *Fritillaria* is now prohibited from Turkey.

Snake's head fritillary (*F. meleagris*) is also widely propagated. It is probably one of the most well known of the fritillaries and is frequently advertised for sale in nursery catalogs. Although this species was once widespread in Europe, it now occurs mostly in southern Europe in scattered colonies. It is extremely rare in the wild in the United Kingdom. Fritillaries are regarded as being relatively easy to grow, provided the gardener takes into consideration the quirks of each species. From seed, the time required to reach flowering size is approximately five years.

FRITILLARIA (Liliaceae)

Species	Category	Notes
F. acmopetala	W, P	Eastern Mediterranean. Wild-collected in Turkey. Propagated in small quantities in the Netherlands. *Fritillaria acmopetala* ssp. *acmopetala* is classified as Rare in Turkey (IUCN).
F. camtschatcensis (Indian rice)	W, P	Northwest Canada and the United States, Japan, Kamchatka (Russia), Kuriles. Wild-collected in Japan. Propagated in small quantities in the United Kingdom, the Netherlands and the United States. Oregon: Threatened. Washington: Sensitive.
F. davisii	P	Southern Greece. Minor commercial collection in Greece. Propagated in small quantities in the Netherlands. Classified as Rare (IUCN) and legally protected in Greece.
F. imperialis (crown imperial)	P	Turkey, Iran, W. Himalaya. Depleted by overcollection but now propagated in the Netherlands by bulblets or by crosscutting at the base; some propagation in Turkey. Cultivars are widely available in trade. Classified as Endangered in Turkey (IUCN).
F. lanceolata (checker-lily)	W, P	British Columbia to Idaho and southern California. Wild-collected and propagated in the United States. Also propagated by meristem culture in the Netherlands.
F. meleagris (snakes's head fritillary)	P	Britain, Europe. Propagated by the millions from seed in the Netherlands. Protected by law in Czechoslovakia, Poland and Hungary.
F. michailovskyi	P	Northeastern Turkey. Propagated in the Netherlands.

F. nigra	See *F. pyrenaica*	
F. pallidiflora	P	Central Asia. Propagated in small quantities in the Netherlands. Classified as Vulnerable (IUCN).
F. persica	P	Turkey to Iran, Israel, and Jordan. Propagated in Israel and the Netherlands; some propagation in Turkey. Classified as Endangered in Turkey (IUCN).
F. pontica	W, P	Greece, Turkey. Wild-collected. Propagated in small quantities in the Netherlands. Protected by law in Greece.
F. pudica (yellow fritillary)	W, P	British Columbia south to Montana, northern California, and Utah. Wild-collected and propagated by seed in the United States. Propagated by meristem culture in the Netherlands.
F. pyrenaica	P	(Syn. *F. nigra*.) France and Italy. Propagated in very small quantities in the Netherlands.

GALANTHUS

Galanthus, the snowdrop, is the most heavily traded wild-collected bulb genus in the world. About 12 species of snowdrops are distributed from southern Europe eastward to Iran. The common snowdrop (*G. nivalis*) has the widest range and has become naturalized in many parts of Europe. The giant snowdrop (*G. elwesii*) also has a fairly large distribution, although excessive collection has caused this species to become quite rare in parts of its range. In the Mediterranean and Black Sea Coast regions of Turkey, in particular, bulbs have been removed from accessible areas and are now found only on steep mountain slopes.

Galanthus nivalis and *G. elwesii* are the two species of *Galanthus* that occur in trade most frequently. *Galanthus nivalis* bulbs in trade are collected from both wild and naturalized populations, primarily in France. During the 1989-1990 commercial season, France exported about 11 million *G. nivalis* bulbs to the Netherlands. The Turkish native *G. elwesii*, however, dominates the trade in snowdrops. Over the past five years, approximately 175 million *Galanthus* bulbs have been exported from Turkey to the Netherlands; most of these bulbs were *G. elwesii*. Other species appear in trade occasionally, usually mixed in with shipments of *G. elwesii* exported from Turkey. Of these species, *G. ikariae* is considered rare, and *G. fosteri* is becoming depleted in Turkey.

Galanthus species are classified in Turkey as vulnerable, and specific measures have been taken to protect the genus. In 1986, the Turkish government set a quota of eight million wild-collected bulbs per year. This move was followed in 1989 by a complete ban on the export of wild-collected bulbs. Also in 1989, the genus *Galanthus* was placed on Appendix II of CITES, an action that requires members of the treaty trading in these species to regulate imports and exports through a system of permits and to restrict trade if species become endangered. In 1992, the quota was reset at 14 million wild-collected bulbs per year.

GALANTHUS (Amaryllidaceae)

Species	Category	Notes
G. elwesii (giant snowdrop)	W, P	Romania, Bulgaria, northern Greece Turkey, Yugoslavia, and west central Asia. Wild-collected in Turkey. Propagated in the Netherlands. Propagation projects in initial stages in Turkey; no propagated stock is yet available. Listed in Appendix II of CITES.
G. fosteri	W	Lebanon, Syria, Turkey. Wild-collected in Turkey; may be included in shipments of *G. elwesii* exported from Turkey. Classified as Vulnerable in Turkey (IUCN). Listed in Appendix II of CITES.

G. gracilis	W	Bulgaria, Greece, Turkey. Wild-collected in Turkey; may be included in shipments of *G. elwesii* exported from Turkey. Classified as Vulnerable in Turkey (IUCN). Listed in Appendix II of CITES.
G. ikariae	W	Greece, Turkey, west central Asia. Wild-collected in Turkey; may be included in shipments of *G. elwesii* exported from Turkey. Propagated in small quantities in the Netherlands. Classified as Vulnerable in Turkey and Rare in Greece (IUCN). Listed in Appendix II of CITES.
G. nivalis (common snowdrop)	W, P	Europe to Turkey; also found naturalized in orchards in the United Kingdom. Wild-collected in Turkey and eastern Europe. Most bulbs harvested from naturalized populations in France. Propagated in the Netherlands and the United Kingdom. Classified as Vulnerable in Turkey (IUCN). Listed in Appendix II of CITES.

IRIS

One of the most colorful genera of bulbous plants, irises were prized by Egyptians for their beauty and by Muslims as a symbol of wealth. Irises have been valued for their reputed medicinal qualities, ranging from removing freckles to healing ulcers; the genus is also well known as the source of orris root, used as a fragrance in cosmetics. *Iris* contains over 200 species distributed throughout the Northern Hemisphere. Plants in this genus are often considered to be rhizomatous or bulbous herbs, rather than bulbs.

Iris are widely cultivated today and are unusual in that they are generally of propagated origin, rather than wild-collected. In addition, irises are primarily grown as cultivars; the number of nurseries devoted to species production is very small.

Vegetative propagation is the most common method of propagation, although many nurseries grow plants from seed. Countries producing large quantities of propagated irises include the Netherlands, the United States, and Israel.

Nevertheless, collection of irises occurs in several countries, in particular Turkey, which exports common iris (*I. germanica*), *I. iberica* ssp. *elegantissima*, *I. paradoxa*, *I. persica*, violet-scented iris (*I. reticulata*), *I. sari*, and *I. tuberosa*. *Iris danfordiae* is now scarce in Turkey but is propagated extensively in the Netherlands. In the United States, many species of native irises are propagated by wildflower nurseries; yet collection is prevalent for some species. In particular, dwarf crested iris (*I. cristata*) and dwarf iris (*I. verna*) are wild-collected; fortunately, both species are quite common. Both *I. tenuis* and dwarf lake iris (*I. lacustris*) are under pressure from loss of habitat and possibly also from overharvest. Both species, however, are also propagated commercially.

In Czechoslovakia, all species of Iris except yellow iris (*I. pseudacorus*) are protected by law. Hungary affords protection to the entire genus.

IRIS (Iridaceae)

Species	Category	Notes
I. atrofusca	P	(Syn. *I. haynei.*) Israel. Propagated in Israel. All exports of *Iris* from Israel are commercially produced.
I. astrachanica	P	Propagated in the United States.
I. atropurpurea	P	Israel, Syria. Propagated in Israel. Classified as Indeterminate in Israel (IUCN).
I. aucheri	P	Southeastern Turkey, northwestern Iran, northern Syria, northern Iraq. Propagated in the United States and the Netherlands.
I. brevicaulis	W, P	Southeastern United States. Some wild-collection may occur but unlikely to be

		commercial. Propagated in the United States; cultivars available. Ohio: protected and listed as Endangered. Oklahoma: Critically Imperiled. Tennessee: protected and listed as Endangered.
I. bucharica	P	Central Asia. Propagated in large quantities in the Netherlands.
I. chamaeiris	P	(Syn. *I. lutescens.*) Southern Europe. Propagated; cultivars available.
I. chrysophylla	W, P	Oregon. Wild-collected but also propagated in the United States; cultivars available.
I. cretensis	P	European form of *I. unguicularis.*
I. cristata (dwarf crested iris)	W, P	Eastern United States. Wild-collected and propagated in the United States. This species is quite widespread; plants in trade largely wild-collected. Maryland: protected and listed as Endangered. Oklahoma: Imperiled. Pennsylvania: protected and listed as Endangered.
I. danfordiae	P	Eastern Turkey. Propagated in large quantities in the Netherlands. Propagated in the United States. Classified as Not Threatened in Turkey (IUCN).
I. delavayi	P	Some propagation in the United States; cultivars available.
I. dichotoma	P	(Syn. *Pardanthopsis dichotoma.*) Manchuria, northern China.
I. douglasiana	W, P	California, Oregon. Propagated; cultivars available. Minor wild-collection occurs.

I. ensata (Japanese iris)	P	(Syn. *I. kaempferi.*) Japan. Propagated in the United States and the Netherlands; cultivars available.
I. foetidissima	P	England and Western Europe. Very common in Europe; considered to be a weed.
I. forrestii	P	Yunnan (China). Propagated; cultivars available.
I. fulva (red iris; copper iris; swamp red iris; red flag)	P	Mississippi Valley. Some propagation in the United States. Cultivars available. Illinois: protected and listed as Threatened. Kentucky: Endangered. Mississippi: Rare (TNC). Tennessee: Special Concern.
I. galatica	P	Central and northern Turkey. Classified as Not Threatened in Turkey (IUCN).
I. gatesii	P	Asia Minor, northern Turkey, northern Iran. Classified as Rare (IUCN).
I. germanica (common iris)	P	Origin unknown; all known plants are found in cultivated or semicultivated state. Exported from Turkey; naturalized in Europe. Cultivars available.
I. glockiana	See *I. suaveolens.*	
I. gracilipes	P	Japan.
I. graminea	P	Central and southern Europe to the Caucasus. Some propagation in the United States.
I. halophila	See *I. spuria.*	
I. haynei	See *I. atrofusca.*	
I. hexagona	P	Southeastern United States. Cultivars available.

I. hispanica	See *I. xiphium.*	
I. histrioides	P	Northeastern Turkey. Propagated in small quantities in the Netherlands; cultivars available. Classified as Rare (IUCN) in Turkey.
I. hoogiana	P	Turkestan. Propagated in small quantities in the Netherlands; cultivars available.
I. iberica ssp. *elegantissima*	W, P	Eastern Turkey, northwestern Iran. Wild-collected in Turkey.
I. innominata	W, P	Southwestern Oregon and California. Wild-collected but also propagated in the United States; cultivars available.
I. japonica	P	Japan, China. Propagated in the Netherlands.
I. kaempferi	See *I. ensata.*	
I. kashmiriana	P	Northern India, Kashmir, Afghanistan. Some propagation in the United States.
I. kerneriana	P	Turkey, Armenia. Some propagation in the United States.
I. lactea	P	Asia. Some propagation in the United States. Cultivars available.
I. lacustris (dwarf lake iris)	W, P	Great Lakes region (United States and Canada). Wild-collected and propagated in the United States. Listed as Threatened under the U.S. Endangered Species Act since 1988. Michigan: protected and listed as Threatened. Wisconsin: protected and listed as Threatened.
I. laevigata	P	East Asia, China, Japan. Some propagation in the United States; cultivars available.

I. loretetii	P	Israel, southern Lebanon. Classified as Endangered (IUCN).
I. lutescens		See *I. chamaeiris*.
I. macrosiphon	P	California, Oregon. Propagated in the United States; cultivars available.
I. magnifica	P	Eastern Europe, west and central Asia. Propagated in the Netherlands; well-known in cultivation. Classified as Indeterminate (IUCN).
I. milesii	W, P	Temperate Himalayas. Wild-collected in India.
I. minutoaurea	P	Japan.
I. missouriensis (western blue flag)	W, P	Northwestern United States; Rocky Mountains. Both propagated and wild-collected.
I. nigricans	P	Jordan, Israel. Propagated in Israel. All *Iris* exported from Israel are commercially produced. Seriously threatened in the wild; classified as Endangered (IUCN) in Jordan.
I. ochroleuca	P	Greece and Turkey. Some propagation in the United States; cultivars available.
I. oncocyclus	W, P	Not a recognized species; rather, a subgenus of *Iris*. Species in this subgenus are native to Asia Minor, Syria and Iran and are characterized by single-flowered stems, peculiar seeds, and diffuse beards. Extensive propagation of cultivars in Israel.
I. orchioides	P	Northeastern Afghanistan, Turkestan. Propagated in the Netherlands.
I. pallida	P	Yugoslavia. Propagated in the United States for over 200 years; numerous cultivars available.

I. pamphylica	P	Southern Turkey. Threatened by specialist collectors. Classified as Rare in Turkey (IUCN).
I. paradoxa	W, P	Armenia, Georgian Republic, northern Iran, Turkey. Wild-collected in Turkey (only *I. paradoxa* forma *choschab* occurs in Turkey). Propagated in the Netherlands. Classified as Vulnerable in Iran and Rare in Turkey (IUCN).
I. persica	W, P	Southern and southeastern Turkey, Iraq, Syria, Lebanon. Exported from Turkey. Propagated in very small quantities in the Netherlands.
I. prismatica (slender blue iris; slender bue flag)	W, P	Eastern North America. Wild-collected and propagated. Delaware: Imperiled. Maine: Threatened. Maryland: protected and listed as Endangered. New Hampshire: protected and listed as Threatened. New York: Critically Imperiled. Pennsylvania: protected and listed as Endangered. Tennessee: Threatened. Virginia: Rare (TNC).
I. pseudacorus (Yellow Iris)	P	England, Europe, western Asia. Propagated in the United States and the Netherlands; cultivars available. Naturalized in the United States.
I. pumila	P	Europe, Asia Minor. Propagated in the United States; cultivars available.
I. purpureobractea	W, P	Western Turkey. Possibly wild-collected on a small scale. Classified as Rare in Turkey (IUCN).
I. reticulata (violet-scented iris)	W, P	Eastern Turkey, the Caucasus, northern Iran, northeastern Iraq. Small quantities exported from Turkey. Propagated in the United States. Propagated by the millions in the Netherlands. Numerous cultivars

		available. Classified as Vulnerable in parts of its range (IUCN).
I. samariae	P	Israel. Propagated in Israel. All *Iris* exported from Israel are commercially produced. Classified as Endangered (IUCN).
I. sanguinea	P	Manchuria, Korea, Japan. Propagated in the United States; cultivars available.
I. sari	W	Asia Minor, central and eastern Turkey. Wild-collected in Turkey. Classified as Not Threatened (IUCN) in Turkey but considered to be vulnerable to collection.
I. setosa	P	Eastern Siberia to Japan, Alaska, Labrador and northeastern North America above Maine. Propagated in the United States.
I. setosa var. *canadensis* (beachhead iris)	P	Labrador to Maine. Propagated in the United States.
I. shrevei	See *I. virginica* var. *shrevei.*	
I. sibirica	P	Central and eastern Europe, western Asia. Propagated in the Netherlands and in the United States; cultivars available. Classified as Rare in Turkey (IUCN). Protected in France.
I. sikkimensis	P	(Syn. *I Clarkei.*) Sikkim. Wild-collected in India.
I. sprengeri	P	Central and southern Turkey. Classified as Endangered in Turkey (IUCN).
I. spuria ssp. *halophila*	P	Central and eastern Europe. Propagated in the United States; cultivars available.
I. stenophylla	P	Southern Turkey. Easy to cultivate.

I. stolonifera	P	Turkey, central Asia.
I. suaveolens	P	(Syn. *I. glockiana.*) Turkey, Bulgaria, Romania, Yugoslavia.
I. susiana (mourning iris)	P	Iran. Exported from Israel, Turkey and Lebanon. In cultivation since the 16th century.
I. tectorum	P	China, Japan. Propagated in the United States.
I. tenax	W, P	Washington, Oregon. Propagated; cultivars available.
I. tenuis	W, P	Oregon. Wild-collected and propagated in the United States.
I. tridentata	P	North Carolina to Florida. Propagated in the United States.
I. tuberosa	W, P	Correct scientific name is *Hermodactylus tuberosus*. Mediterranean. Propagated in the United States. Wild-collected in Turkey from both wild and naturalized populations.
I. unguicularis	P	Mediterranean. Propagated; cultivars available.
I. verna (dwarf iris)	W, P	Pennsylvania to Kentucky and Georgia. Wild-collected but also propagated by a few firms. Plants offered are primarily of wild origin. Maryland: protected and listed as Endangered. Ohio: protected and listed as Threatened. Pennsylvania: protected and listed as Threatened.
I. versicolor (blue flag)	W, P	Eastern Canada to Pennsylvania and Minnesota. Wild-collected and propagated in the United States. Cultivars available. Virginia: Imperiled.
I. virginica (southern blue flag)	W, P	Southeastern United States west to Texas. Propagated in the United

		States; cultivars available. Oklahoma: Imperiled.
I. virginica var. *shrevei*	W, P	Central United States. Both wild-collected and propagated in the United States. Kansas: Imperiled.
I. warlsind	—	Not a recognized species. Iris "Warlsind" is a hybrid between *I. warleyensis* and *I. aucheri.*
I. winogradowii	P	Caucasus. Propagated and established in cultivation. Classified as Indeterminate (IUCN).
I. xiphioides (English iris)	P	Pyrenees and northwestern Spain. Propagated in the Netherlands; cultivars available.
I. xiphium (Spanish iris)	P	(Syn. *I. hispanica.*) Southern France, Portugal, Spain, North Africa. Propagated in Israel; many cultivars available.

LEUCOJUM

Leucojum, also known as snowflake, consists of approximately 10 species distributed throughout Europe to the western Mediterranean. The most widespread species, *L. aestivum* or the summer snowflake, occurs in southeastern England and central Europe and has been cultivated since 1759. Snowflakes appear quite similar to snowdrops, both having white flowers and narrow leaves. However, *Leucojum*'s perianth parts (that is, the sepals and the petals) are of even length, whereas *Galanthus* has sepals much shorter than the inner ring of petals.

Most *Leucojum* bulbs in trade are of wild origin. The government of Turkey has set an export quota of five million wild-collected *Leucojum* bulbs per year. Even so, in the 1988-1989 commercial season, Turkey exceeded the quota and exported over eight million *Leucojum* bulbs, most of which were summer snowflake (*L. aestivum*). Some artificial propagation of *L. aestivum* is being carried out in Turkey, however only on a small scale. Spring snowflake (*L. vernum*) is primarily collected from the wild in Hungary, although growers in the Netherlands produce this species on a very minor scale. *Leucojum* are protected by law in Czechoslovakia.

While few *Leucojum* species bulbs are propagated on a large scale, the appealing 'Gravetye Giant,' a selection of *L. aestivum*, is propagated extensively. This plant is a solid choice for the garden; it is a robust plant that flowers freely.

LEUCOJUM (Amaryllidaceae)

Species	Category	Notes
L. aestivum ssp. *aestivum* (summer snowflake)	W, P	Europe to southwestern Asia. Widely cultivated and naturalized. Wild-collected in Turkey. Propagated in small quantities in the Netherlands and the United Kingdom, but not on a commercial scale. Classified as Vulnerable in Turkey (IUCN).
L. autumnale (autumn snowflake)	W	Portugal, Spain, Sardinia, Sicily, North Africa. Previously wild-collected in Portugal. Propagated in the United Kingdom but not on a commercial scale.
L. 'Gravetye'	P	Not a recognized species; rather, a form of *L. aestivum* known as 'Gravetye Giant'.
L. roseum	W	Corsica and Sardinia. Considered Rare on Sardinia (IUCN).
L. vernum (spring snowflake)	W, P	Southern and eastern Europe. Most wild stock is collected from eastern Europe. Propagated in the United Kingdom and in the thousands in the Netherlands. Protected by law in Poland.

LILIUM

The genus *Lilium* consists of 80 to 90 species distributed throughout the north temperate zone. China, in particular, has a wealth of lily species and a long history of lily cultivation. Some historians estimate that madonna lily (*L. candidum*) has been in cultivation for 3,000 years, its curative powers valued in the treatment of boils, corns, and dropsy. Since the 10th century, several lily species have been grown in Chinese gardens, for medicine and food as well as for ornamental purposes.

Lilies are propagated on an enormous scale in the United States, the Netherlands, France, Japan, and Israel. Propagation methods include division of offsets and of bulb scales; some species even produce aerial bulblets that can grow into flowering size plants within three years. Most of the propagation involves the cultivation of hybrids; however, growers are now beginning to put more energy into cultivars.

Although commercial cultivation of lilies is quite extensive, some species continue to be collected from the wild. It is likely that the biggest threat to species lilies is from specialist collectors. *Lilium* are protected by law in Czechoslovakia.

LILIUM (Liliaceae)

Species	Category	Notes
L. canadense (wild yellow lily; Canada lily)	W, P	Eastern North America. Primarily wild-collected; propagated in very small quantities in the United States. Propagation is very slow by seed and division. Alabama: Critically Imperiled. Delaware: Critically Imperiled. Indiana: protected and listed as Threatened. Kansas: *L. canadense* var. *michiganense* is listed as Critically Imperiled. Rhode Island: Threatened. South Carolina: Of Concern. South Dakota: *L. canadense* ssp. *michiganense* is listed as Critically Rare. Tennessee: Threatened.

L. canadensis	—	Not a recognized species. Probably refers to *L. canadense*.
L. candidum (madonna lily)	W, P	Exact origin unknown; presumed to be native to the Mediterranean region. Bulbs are exported from Israel and Turkey. Widely cultivated; propagated in Israel, Poland, and the Netherlands. Also propagated in small quantities in Turkey, resulting largely from reduced availability of wild plants. Cultivars available. Classified as Endangered in Turkey (IUCN); protected by law in Greece.
L. carolinianum	See *L. catesbaei.*	
L. catesbaei (southern red lily)	W	(Syn. *L. carolinianum*.). Southeastern United States. Wild-collected. Florida: protected and listed as Threatened; Rare (TNC). Louisiana: Critically Imperiled. Virginia: Critically Imperiled.
L. citronella	P	Not a species; "Citronella" is one of the Asiatic hybrids.
L. hansonii (Japanese turk's cap)	P	Korea. Propagated in the Netherlands and Japan.
L. henryi	P	Central China. Propagated in the Netherlands and Taiwan.
L. maculatum	?	Japan. Not common in cultivation.
L. martagon (martagon lily; turk's cap)	W, P	Europe and western Asia. Introduced 1596. Easy to grow, naturalizes readily. Propagated in the Netherlands. Wild-collected in France. Export from Turkey banned since 1986. Classified as Endangered in Turkey (IUCN); protected by law in Poland.

L. michauxii (turk's cap lily)	W, P	Virginia to Florida and Louisiana. The majority of plants in trade are of wild origin; propagated in small quantities in the United States. Propagation by seed and division is quite slow. Florida: Critically Imperiled. West Virginia: Critically Imperiled.
L. michiganense (Michigan lily)	W, P	Ontario south to Tennessee, Arkansas, and Kansas. Majority of specimens are wild-collected, as propagation is very slow from seed and division. Some taxonomists believe this taxon is a variation of *L. canadense.* Mississippi: Critically Imperiled. New York: protected and listed as Endangered; Critically Imperiled. Tennessee: Threatened.
L. pardalinum (leopard lily)	W, P	Oregon and California. Wild-collected and propagated in the United States.
L. philadelphicum (wood lily)	W, P	Maine to Ontario, south to Kentucky. Wild-collected and propagated in the United States. Propagation is quite slow. Alabama: Critically Imperiled. Colorado: Rare. Delaware: Extirpated. Kentucky: Threatened. Maryland: protected and listed as Endangered; Extirpated. New Mexico: *L. philadelphicum* var. *andinum* is protected and listed as Endangered. New Jersey: Rare (TNC). Ohio: protected and listed as Endangered. Tennessee: protected and listed as Endangered.
L. regale (regal lily; royal lily)	P	Western China. Propagated in the Netherlands by the millions.
L. superbum (American turk's cap lily)	W, P	New Hampshire to Georgia and Alabama. Wild-collected and propagated in the United States. Propagation is easy but slow. Alabama: Rare (TNC). Florida: Critically

		Imperiled. Illinois: protected and listed as Endangered. Indiana: protected and listed as Threatened. Kentucky: Endangered. Mississippi: Rare (TNC). New Hampshire: protected and listed as Endangered. Ohio: Potentially Threatened.
L. washingtonianum (Washington lily)	W, P	California. Wild-collected and propagated in the United States. Very difficult and slow to propagate; most plants in trade are wild-collected.

MUSCARI

Most gardeners are familiar with *Muscari*, the grape hyacinth, a bulb that increases rapidly and easily, sometimes to the point of being a nuisance. The genus is large, consisting of approximately 40 species, and its taxonomy is somewhat unclear. Some specialists believe that *Muscari* should be divided into four genera, *Leopoldia, Botryanthus, Muscarimia,* and *Pseudomuscari,* while others prefer to put all species under *Muscari* and to separate the genus into subgenera or sections. For the sake of simplicity, all species are grouped together here under the single genus name of *Muscari.*

Muscari is native to the Mediterranean and southwestern Asia. Grape hyacinths are easy to grow and quite hardy. Propagation by offsets is the easiest method to increase stock, but seed propagation is also not difficult, as *Muscari* sets seed freely and germinates readily. From seed, a bulb of flowering size can be produced in three years.

Muscari bulbs are propagated extensively, and numerous cultivars are appealing and widely available. Even so, various *Muscari* species merit protection in certain parts of their range. For example, Poland protects tassel hyacinth (*M. comosum)* and common grape hyacinth (*M. botryoides*), and Hungary protects *M. botryoides.* Czechoslovakia affords protection to the entire genus, and Turkey has banned the export of wild specimens of *Muscari.*

MUSCARI (Liliaceae)

Species	Category	Notes
M. album	–	Not a recognized species. Plants offered under this name are cultivars of *M. conicum, M. botryoides,* or *M. armeniacum.*
M. armeniacum	P	Turkey. Propagated extensively in the Netherlands. Numerous selections available: 'Blue Spike,' 'Cantab,' and 'Album.'
M. aucheri	W, P	Turkey, Asia Minor. Wild-collected in Turkey. Propagated in the Netherlands.
M. azureum	P	Eastern Turkey, Caucasus. Propagated in small quantities in the Netherlands.
M. botryoides (common grape hyacinth)	P	Central and southeastern Europe. Several selections are offered by nurseries, including 'Album' Propagated in the United States. *M. botryoides album* propagated in the Netherlands. Also offered are 'Carneum' and 'Pallidum.' Protected by law in Poland, Hungary, and France.
M. comosum (tassel hyacinth)	W, P	Southern and central Europe. Introduced 1596. Propagated in the Netherlands. *M. comosum* var. *plumosum* also propagated in the Netherlands. This variation has sterile flowers. Wild-collected in Turkey. Protected in France.
M. latifolium	P	Southern and western Turkey. Propagated in the Netherlands.
M. longipes	W	Turkey, Caucasus, Iran and Iraq. Wild-collected in Turkey.
M. neglectum	W, P	North Africa, Europe, the Orient. Wild-collected in Turkey. Propagated in the Netherlands. Bulbs produce many offsets and spread rapidly.

M. tenuiflorum	W	Central Europe, Near Orient, Ukraine. Wild-collected in Turkey.
M. tubergenianum	P	Iran. Propagated in the Netherlands. Introduced in 1940 by Van Tubergen, considered to be either a cultivar of *M. aucheri* or a hybrid between *M. aucheri* x *M. armeniacum*.

NARCISSUS

When gardeners think of the plight of bulbs in the wild, the delicate miniature daffodils are sure to come to mind. Native to Europe, northern Africa, and western Asia, *Narcissus* is a genus that has been cultivated for centuries. Authorities believe there are approximately 60 species, but the taxonomy of the genus is quite confusing. Most species naturalize readily, making it difficult to determine their origins, especially those of southeastern France and northern Italy. In addition, *Narcissus* species hybridize very easily, which makes species identification even more difficult.

Most of the *Narcissus* in trade are propagated hybrids and cultivars. Horticulturists in the Netherlands and in the United Kingdom, in particular, have devoted much effort to producing gorgeous, sturdy daffodils with enchanting colors and contrasts. Yet with the growing interest in miniature flowers and rock and woodland gardens, many consumers have turned to the miniature species daffodils. These elegant bulbs with their tiny exquisite blossoms originate for the most part in Spain and Portugal, and to a lesser extent in Turkey and Morocco. Collection of wild species has occurred not only to satisfy general gardening tastes but also to supply collectors and horticulturists with the wild plants required for breeding.

Many of the native *Narcissus* species in Spain and Portugal are under pressure from habitat loss as well as from collection. *Narcissus cyclamineus* is classified as Rare and *N. asturiensis* as Indeterminate in Portugal by IUCN; both are included in a list of plants recommended for protection. *Narcissus willkommii* recently may have become extinct in the wild in Spain as a result of construction activities, although plants are being introduced into cultivation in a safer area. *Narcissus calcicola, N. cantabricus,* and *N. scaberulus* may be vulnerable to collection pressure, and *N. viridiflorus* has become extremely rare because of habitat destruction and overcollection. The most frequent *Narcissus* export from Turkey, *N. tazetta,* is both wild-collected and artificially propagated in Turkey. *Narcissus serotinus* is considered to be Rare in Turkey by IUCN. The government of Turkey has imposed an export quota of 500,000 wild bulbs for the entire genus.

As a result of increasing regulations limiting the harvest of *Narcissus* and pressure from conservationists and concerned gardeners, horticulturists are concentrating on propagation of the miniature narcissus. Many of the species are considered temperamental, although that reputation may have developed because imported wild-collected bulbs arrive in such a sorry state after a lengthy storage and transport period that survival is often a miracle regardless of the gardener's skills. Growers especially in the Netherlands, but also in the United States, who are beginning to propagate *Narcissus* species are also attempting to produce miniature hybrids and cultivars that will withstand the rigors of life in the north temperate zone, where temperatures frequently drop below freezing.

Propagation of *Narcissus* is most rapid by lifting and dividing; offsets reach flowering size in two years. Seed propagation is regarded as the best method for increasing species bulbs, requiring approximately three to four years for a plant to reach commercial size. To develop a successful hybrid, however, the time commitment is much longer. Hybridization experiments must be followed through several generations to get the best shapes, sizes, and colors, as well as the traits that will ensure a sturdy plant. After each hybridization, the horticulturist must wait for the plant to reach maturity before additional pollination experiments can be carried out. Then the plant has to set seed, the seed must germinate, and the cycle can begin anew. Some horticulturists report that at least 10 to 15 years are necessary to produce a reliable hybrid.

NARCISSUS (Amaryllidaceae)

Species	Category	Notes
N. asturiensis	W, P	(Syn. *N. minimus.*) Portugal, Spain. Frequently still listed in catalogs as *N. minimus* or, erroneously, as *N. asturiensis minimus*. Wild-collected in Portugal. Propagated in very small quantities in the Netherlands; some specialist growers in the United States are starting to propagate this species. Classified as Indeterminate (IUCN).
N. bulbocodium ssp. *bulbocodium* (hoop-petticoat daffodil)	W, P	Spain, Portugal, France. Although thought to be temperamental, this species increases readily in the southeastern United States. However, the majority of bulbs are wild-collected; specialist growers are producing extremely small quantities.
N. bulbocodium var. *conspicuus* (large flower hoop-petticoat daffodil)	W, P	According to *Flora Europaea*, this species should now be referred to as *N. bulbocodium* ssp. *bulbocodium* var. *conspicuus*; under new nomenclature, this includes *N. bulbocodium* var. *tenuifolius*. Propagation has started in the Netherlands, but the bulbs are unlikely to have reached commercial size yet.
N. bulbocodium tenuifolius	See entry for *N. bulbocodium conspicuus.*	
N. canaliculatus	P	Mediterranean. Propagated in the Netherlands and southern France. Taxonomy is rather confusing; some say that this species is *N. italicus* var. *lacticolor*, while others believe it to be a dwarf form of *N. tazetta*.
N. cyclamineus	W	Portugal, Spain. Used extensively for hybridizing, Propagated by specialist growers in the Netherlands and the United Kingdom; not produced on a

		commercial scale. Many cultivars of *N. cyclamineus*, however, are propagated in the Netherlands. Classified as Rare (IUCN).
N. jonquilla (common jonquil)	P	Spain, Portugal. Propagated in the Netherlands. Classified as Indeterminate (IUCN).
N. juncifolius	See *N. requienii.*	
N. minimus	See *N. asturiensis.*	
N. minor	P	Southwestern France, northern Spain. Much confusion over the nomenclature of this species: some believe it to be a hybrid between *N. asturiensis* and *N. pseudonarcissus*; others regard it as a distinct species and say that it was formerly known as *N. nanus*, which is now propagated in the Netherlands. Several cultivars are available, such as *N. minor* 'Pumilus Plenus' which is otherwise known as *N.* 'Rip van Winkle.'
N. minor pumilus	See *N. pumilus.*	
N. obvallaris	P	Western Europe. Some authorities now call this plant *N. pseudonarcissus* ssp. *obvallaris*. Propagated in the Netherlands under the name *N. obvallaris*. Not really a miniature daffodil, it reaches a height of 10 to 12 inches. Used in hybridizing. Propagated in large quantities (over 1 million) in the Netherlands.
N. poeticus ssp. *poeticus* (poet's narcissus)	P	France, Spain, Italy, Greece. Numerous cultivars available.
N. pseudonarcissus (trumpet narcissus)	W, P	Western Europe. The most propagated of all *Narcissus* species, yet still wild-collected in Belgium. Extensively naturalized in Europe.

N. pseudonarcissus obvallaris	—	Wales. See entry for *N. obvallaris*.
N. pumilis	P	Portugal. Also referred to as *N. minor* var. *pumilus*. Propagated in the Netherlands.
N. recurvus	P	(Syn. *N. poeticus* ssp. *poeticus* var. *recurvus*.) France, Spain, Italy, Greece. Propagated in the Netherlands.
N. requienii	W	(Syn. *N. juncifolius*.) Southern France, Spain. Wild-collected.
N. romieuxii	W, P	North Africa. Wild-collected. Propagated in extremely small quantities by specialist growers in the United States. Majority of bulbs are wild-collected.
N. rupicola ssp. *rupicola*	W, P	North and central Spain, north and central Portugal. Wild-collected in Portugal. Propagated in extremely small quantities by specialist growers in the United States. Majority of bulbs are wild-collected.
N. scaberulus	W, P	Portugal. Wild-collected in Portugal. Very restricted distribution. Propagated in extremely small quantities by specialist growers in the United States. Majority of bulbs are wild-collected. Classified as Vulnerable (IUCN).
N. tazetta lacticolor	W	Mediterranean. *N. tazetta* ssp. *lacticolor*. Wild-collected.
N. triandrus ssp. *triandrus* (angel's tears)	W, P	North and central Spain, north and central Portugal, northwestern France. According to *Flora Europaea*, *N. triandrus* var. *albus*, *N. triandrus* var. *cernuus*, and *N. triandrus* var. *pulchellus* are now included in *N. triandrus* ssp. *triandrus*. Most triandrus are short-lived; therefore, stock is maintained by wild-

		collection. Propagated in very small quantities in the Netherlands; used extensively in hybridizing. Many cultivars available. Propagated in extremely small quantities by specialist growers in the United States. Majority of bulbs are wild-collected.
N. triandrus albus	W	(Syn. *N. triandrus* ssp. *triandrus.*) Wild-collected in Portugal. See entry for *N. triandrus.*
N. triandrus concolor	W	(Syn. *N. triandrus* ssp. *pallidus.*) Wild-collected in Portugal.
N. triandrus pulchellus	W	See *N. triandrus* ssp. *triandrus.* Wild-collected in Portugal.
N. watieri	W, P	Morocco, Atlas Mountains. Although used for hybridizing, stock is wild-collected. Propagated in extremely small quantities by specialist growers in the United States. Majority of bulbs are wild-collected.

ORNITHOGALUM

About 100 species of *Ornithogalum* occur from Europe through western Asia to Africa. Approximately 20 of these species are cultivated, ranging from the well-known star-of-Bethlehem (*O. umbellatum*) to the chincherinchee (*O. thyrsoides*) of South Africa, a favorite in florist's bouquets. While some *Ornithogalum* are hardy and others quite tender, they all seem to increase extremely rapidly. Both the nodding star-of-Bethlehem (*O. nutans*) and *O. umbellatum* are widely naturalized in the eastern United States. *Ornithogalum umbellatum* takes over easily and is considered to be an invasive species.

Ornithogalum are easily propagated and increase most rapidly by offsets. Seed propagation is also feasible, and a flowering size plant can be expected within three to four years after germination. Numerous species of this genus are propagated in the Netherlands, the United States, and Israel. In South Africa, there is much experimentation with hybrids, as well as a thriving cut flower industry based on *O. thyrsoides*. This species is particularly valued as a cut flower because it ships so well. Stems can be cut when in bud, shipped by sea from South Africa to Europe, and upon arrival will be ready to bloom.

ORNITHOGALUM (Liliaceae)

Species	Category	Notes
O. arabicum (Arabian star-of-Bethlehem)	P	Mediterranean. Propagated in the Netherlands, Israel, South Africa, and in small quantities in the United States.
O. nutans (nodding star-of-Bethlehem)	W, P	Southern Europe, southwest Asia. Wild-collected in Turkey. Propagated in the Netherlands. Naturalized in many countries, including the eastern part of the United States. Widely cultivated.
O. saundersiae (giant chincherinchee)	P	Natal, eastern Transvaal (South Africa), Swaziland. Extremely poisonous; has been subject to eradication programs in the past. Propagated as both an ornamental and a cut flower in South Africa. Also propagated in the Netherlands and the United States.
O. tenuifolium	W	Mediterranean, France, Russia.
O. thyrsoide (wonderflower; chincherinchee)	P	Southwestern Cape Province (South Africa). Extremely poisonous; has been subject to eradication programs in the past. Propagated in the Netherlands and the United States. Cultivated for the cut flower industry; several cultivars available.

O. umbellatum (star-of-Bethlehem)	W, P	Europe, North Africa. Wild-collected in Turkey. Propagated in the Netherlands and the United States. Widely naturalized in Europe and the eastern United States.

PUSCHKINIA

A small genus native to Asia Minor and the Caucasus, *Puschkinia* was named after the famous Russian botanist, Count Apollo Apollosvich Mussin-Puschkin. Some botanists consider the most commonly grown species, the striped squill (*P. scilloides*), to be the only species in the genus and the other species frequently listed in catalogs, *P. libanotica* and P. alba, to be forms of the species. If this is indeed the case, *P. libanotica* is the blue form of *P. scilloides*, and *P. libanotica alba*, or *P. alba*, is the white form.

Puschkinia is quite easy to propagate. Propagation by offsets is the most rapid method of increasing stock; bulbs can reach flowering size in one season. Propagation by seed requires two growing seasons to produce a flowering size plant. Given the ease of propagation, it is not surprising that *Puschkinia* is propagated extensively in the Netherlands.

PUSCHKINIA (Liliaceae)

Species	Category	Notes
P. alba	See *P. scilloides*.	
P. libanotica	See *P. scilloides*.	
P. scilloides (striped squill)	P	Turkey, Caucasus, Iran to Lebanon. There are two forms of *P. scilloides*: the blue form is often listed as *P. libanotica* and the white form as *P. libanotica alba* or *P. alba*. The blue form is propagated extensively (in the millions) in the Netherlands. The white form is also propagated in the Netherlands, although to a much lesser extent.

SCILLA

Scilla, commonly known as squill, is a large genus of approximately 90 species occurring in Africa, Asia, and Europe. This genus is sometimes confused with sea squill (*Urginea maritima*), whose bulbs are used to manufacture rat poison. *Scilla* is closely related to *Urginea* and likewise contains several species with bulbs that are extremely toxic.

Scilla are widely cultivated and relatively easy to propagate. Propagation by offsets and by seed is readily achieved, but some species produce few offsets. If seed propagation is carried out, flowering size plants can be expected in three to four years.

All species of *Scilla* are protected in Hungary, and in Turkey all *Scilla* are considered to be Rare by IUCN. In addition, Turkey has set an export quota of 275,000 wild bulbs per year for twinleaf squill (*S. bifolia*). Numerous *Scilla* species are propagated, and many cultivars have been developed.

SCILLA (Liliaceae)

Species	Category	Notes
S. biflora	—	Not a recognized species; most likely is a misspelling of *S. bifolia*.
S. bifolia (twinleaf squill)	W, P	Central and southern Europe to Asia Minor. Wild-collected in Turkey; an export quota has been set for 275,000 wild bulbs per year. Propagated in the Netherlands.
S. campanulata	P	Spain, Portugal. Now known as *Hyacinthoides hispanica* but often listed in catalogs as *S. campanulata* or *S. hispanica*. Propagated in the Netherlands. Many cultivars available.
S. hispanica	See *S. campanulata*.	
S. hyacinthoides	P	Mediterranean region, Portugal. Protected in France.

S. litardierei (*meadow squill*)	P	(Syn. *S. pratensis, S. amethystina.*) Western Yugoslavia. Propagated under the name *S. pratensis* in the Netherlands. Classified as Rare (IUCN).
S. natalensis (blue squill; wild squill)	P	Natal, Cape Province, Transvaal, Orange Free State (South Africa). Relatively easy to propagate; propagated by division in very small quantities in the United States. Collected from the wild by the hundreds of thousands each year for use in traditional medicine in South Africa. No evidence of collection for the horticultural market.
S. paradoxum	—	Not a recognized species.
S. peruviana (Cuban lily; Peruvian jacinth)	P	Portugal, Spain, Italy, northern Africa. Propagated in small quantities in the Netherlands and the United States.
S. pratensis	See *S. litardieri.*	
S. scilloides (Chinese squill; Japanese jacinth)	?	(Syn. *S. chinensis, S. japonica)* Korea, China, Taiwan, Japan.
S. siberica (Siberian squill)	P	(Syn. *S. cernua.*) Northern Iran, Asia Minor to the Caucasus. Extensive propagation in the Netherlands. Numerous cultivars available, including 'Alba', 'Azurea', 'Taurica' and 'Spring Beauty.'
S. tubergeniana	P	Iran, the Caucasus. Propagated in the Netherlands. Correct name for the species is now *S. mischtschenkoana*; however, the name *S. tubergeniana* is used far more widely.

STERNBERGIA

The genus *Sternbergia*, the winter daffodil, consists of eight or nine species with a distribution centered in Turkey, the Caucasus, and western Iran. Some of these species are considered rare or threatened, including *S. candida, S. clusiana, S. fischeriana*, and *S. pulchella*, while the status of species with widespread distributions is either not threatened (*S. colchiflora, S. sicula*) or unknown (*S. alexandrae, S. lutea*).

Sternbergia is concentrated in Turkey, and it is in this country that the majority of bulbs are collected for export. The Turkish government has banned the export of all wild-collected native *S. candida*. Nevertheless, bulbs continue to be exported, often labeled as propagated when in fact they have been transplanted from the wild. *Sternbergia* are classified by IUCN as Vulnerable in Turkey, and *S. candida* is considered Endangered in Turkey.

Sternbergia lutea is the species most commonly found in trade, although *S. clusiana* is becoming more frequent since it is often collected and mislabeled as *S. lutea*. Also exported from Turkey are *S. fischeriana* and *S. sicula*. Unlike the easily artificially propagated *S. lutea, S. clusiana* rarely survives in gardens. Although *S. lutea* increases rapidly vegetatively and may now be cultivated in the Netherlands and the United Kingdom, most stock is still collected from the wild. *S. clusiana* likewise is primarily wild-collected.

Cultivation of all species of *Sternbergia* is regarded as difficult, but several specialist nurseries are beginning to propagate *S. candida, S. clusiana, S. sicula*, and *S. lutea*. Some countries have taken measures to protect *Sternbergia* in the wild; for example, both Turkey and Israel protect the genus. *Sternbergia colchiflora* is protected in Hungary and in France. Also, in 1989, the genus was added to Appendix II of CITES. An Appendix II listing does not prohibit trade, but regulations require that shipments be accompanied by an export permit and that species not be traded if trade is detrimental to the status of the species in the wild.

STERNBERGIA (Amaryllidaceae)

Species	Category	Notes
S. candida	W	Southwestern Turkey. Species discovered in 1976; wild populations have already decreased due to overcollection. Propagated in small quantities in the United Kingdom; most available stock is of wild origin. Classified as Endangered in Turkey (IUCN). Listed in Appendix II of CITES.
S. clusiana	W	Southern Turkey, Syria, Lebanon, Iraq, Iran. Wild-collected in Turkey. Often exported under the name of *S. lutea*. Propagated in small quantities in Europe; most available stock is of wild origin. Classified as Vulnerable in Turkey (IUCN). Listed in Appendix II of CITES.
S. fischeriana	W, P	Turkey, the Caucasus, Iraq, Iran, Syria. Wild-collected in Turkey. Propagated in very small quantities by specialist growers in the Netherlands; most available stock is of wild origin. Classified as Vulnerable in Turkey (IUCN). Listed in Appendix II of CITES.
S. lutea (winter daffodil; lily of the field)	W	Mediterranean region, central Asia. Wild-collected in India and Turkey. Propagated in small quantities in the United Kingdom, the United States and the Netherlands; most available stock is of wild origin. In recent years, exports of *S. lutea* from Turkey have turned out to be *S. clusiana* or *S. candida*. Classified as Vulnerable in Turkey (IUCN). Listed in Appendix II of CITES.
S. sicula	W	Southern Italy, southwestern Turkey, southern Greece and Crete. Wild-collected in Turkey. Propagated in small quantities in Europe; most avail-

		able stock is of wild origin. Classified as Vulnerable in Turkey (IUCN). Listed in Appendix II of CITES.
S. s. graeca	—	Not a recognized variation or subspecies.

TRILLIUM

Trillium is one of our best-loved woodland wildflowers. Consisting of about 40 species distributed throughout North America and eastern Asia, this genus has been a garden favorite for decades. Many species have beautiful large leaves, and some can reach a height of two feet. A wide selection of *Trillium* is offered in catalogs and from roadside wildflower stands. The vast majority of these plants are wild-collected.

Propagation of *Trillium* has been hindered by the length of time required. In general, horticulturists find that four to seven years are needed for a seed-grown plant to reach flowering size. The time span, as well as the expense involved, has kept the market in wild-collected plants active. Some small nurseries are attempting to produce propagated trilliums on a commercial scale, but the number of brokers selling wild plants far exceeds the meager quantity of propagated plants. The practice of transplanting wild plants to nursery beds before sale has become a contentious issue. Several nurseries have labeled transplanted specimens as "nursery grown," when in fact the plants were collected from the wild. Overwintering in a nursery does not transform a collected plant into a propagated one.

Trillium is not propagated on a commercial scale in Europe, although some success has been reported in micropropagation. In general, North American plants available for sale in Europe and Japan have been wild-collected in the United States and Canada.

It should be noted that much taxonomic confusion exists concerning this genus. In preparing this guide, every attempt has been made to sort out the synonymy so that the reader can locate the desired species description.

TRILLIUM (Liliaceae)

Species	Category	Notes
T. album	—	Not a recognized species.
T. catesbaei (rosy wake-robin)	W, P	(Syn. *T. stylosum, T. nervosum.*) North Carolina to Georgia and Alabama. Primarily wild-collected; propagated in very small quantities.
T. cernuum (nodding trillium; sugar berry; smiling wake-robin)	W	Eastern North America. Wild-collected in the United States. Propagation from seed and division is possible but slow. Delaware: Imperiled. Illinois: protected and listed as Endangered. Indiana: *T. cernuum* var. *macranthum* is protected and listed as Endangered. Ohio: Presumed Extirpated. South Dakota: Rare. West Virginia: Critically Imperiled.
T. chloropetalum (giant trillium)	W	Washington to California. Propagated in very small quantities by specialist growers, but propagation is very slow.
T. cuneatum (little sweet trillium)	W	Southeastern United States. Illinois: protected and listed as Endangered.
T. decumbens (trailing trillium)	W	Southeastern United States. Restricted range. Alabama: Rare (TNC). Tennessee: protected and listed as Endangered.
T. discolor	See *T. sessile* var. *wrayi.*	
T. erectum (purple trillium)	W	Southern Ontario and Quebec, south to North Carolina and Georgia. Wild-collected in the United States. Propagation from seed and division is possible but slow. Harvested from the wild for medicinal purposes. Illinois: protected and listed as Endangered. Rhode Island: Threatened.

T. flexipes (drooping trillium; nodding trillium)	W	Central and northern United States. Maryland: protected and listed as Endangered. Mississippi: Critically Imperiled. New York: protected and listed as Vulnerable. Pennsylvania: Rare (TNC). West Virginia: Critically Imperiled.
T. grandiflorum (white wake-robin; large-flowered trillium)	W, P	(Syn. *T. rhomboideum* var. *grandiflorum.*) Quebec to Minnesota, south to South Carolina and Georgia. Primarily wild-collected. Propagated in small quantities in Europe. Maine: Possibly Extirpated.
T. luteum	See *T. viride* var. *luteum*.	
T. nivale (snow trillium, dwarf trillium)	W, P	Pennsylvania to Minnesota, south to Missouri and Nebraska. Primarily wild-collected. Georgia: protected and listed as Threatened. Kentucky: Endangered. Maryland: protected and listed as Endangered. Michigan: protected and listed as Threatened. Minnesota: Special Concern. Ohio: Potentially Threatened. Pennsylvania: Rare (TNC). South Dakota: Rare. West Virginia: Imperiled. Wisconsin: protected and listed as Threatened.
T. ovatum (coast trillium)	W, P	British Columbia. Both propagated and wild-collected.
T. recurvatum (purple trillium; reflexed trillium)	W	Michigan to Iowa, south to Alabama and Mississippi. Wild-collected in the United States. Propagation from seed and division is possible but slow. Alabama: Imperiled. Louisiana: Imperiled. Michigan: protected and listed as Threatened. Ohio: Potentially Threatened.
T. rivale (brook trillium)	W	Southern Oregon and northern California. Classified as Rare (IUCN). Protected by law in California.

T. sessile (toadshade)	W	Eastern North America. Wild-collected in the United States. Propagation from seed and division is possible but slow. *T. sessile* var. *wrayi* (syn. *T. discolor*) is also wild-collected. Alabama: Imperiled. Michigan: protected and listed as Threatened. New York: protected and listed as Endangered; Critically Imperiled. North Carolina: protected and listed as Threatened.
T. stylosum	See *T. catesbaei.*	
T. undulatum (painted trillium)	W	Quebec and Manitoba south to Georgia, Tennessee, and South Carolina. Wild-collected in the United States. Propagation from seed and division is possible but slow. Kentucky: Threatened. Michigan: protected and listed as Endangered. New Jersey: Rare (TNC). Ohio: protected and listed as Threatened.
T. vaseyi (Vasey's trillium)	W	Southern Appalachian Mountains. Wild-collected in the United States. Propagation by seed and division is possible but slow. Alabama: Critically Imperiled.
T. viride (wood trillium; green trillium)	W, P	Kansas and Illinois, to Oklahoma and Arkansas. Primarily wild-collected. *T. viride* var. *luteum* occurs in South Carolina, Georgia, Kentucky, and Florida. Illinois: protected and listed as Threatened. Michigan: protected and listed as Possibly Extirpated.

TULIPA

Tulipa is the most well-known of all the bulb genera. Almost everyone, even those who have never picked up a trowel, knows what a tulip is. This is not surprising, given the genus's long and fascinating history. About 100 species of tulips are found throughout Europe, western and central Asia, and northern Africa, with a center of distribution in Iran, Turkey, Afghanistan, Uzbekistan, and Turkmenistan. It is in this region that tulips were first brought into cultivation, and here also that they were given the name of "toliban," which means "turban" in Persian.

Tulips were first introduced to the west in 1572 when Ogier Ghiselin de Busbecq, the ambassador from the Holy Roman Empire to Suleiman the Magnificent, sent some bulbs and seeds to the French botanist Clusius. Clusius, then working in Austria, was appointed professor of botany at Leiden in the Netherlands. He carried the tulips with him to his new post. Although many of the bulbs were planted in Leiden, many others were stolen and subsequently distributed throughout the Netherlands.

Tulips became so popular in their new home that horticulturists devoted boundless energy to propagation and experimentation, though, even prior to the tulip's introduction to Europe, many tulip cultivars and hybrids were already in existence. The Netherlands soon became the world's foremost producer of tulips, a position it still holds. Today, thousands of cultivars and hybrids are available to gardeners, many of them derived from just a few species, in particular *Tulipa gesneriana, T. greigii, T. fosteriana* , and the waterlily tulip (*T. kaufmanniana*).

The vast majority of gardeners plant the beautiful hybrids and cultivars produced in the Netherlands and increasingly in western North America. Nevertheless, there is a market for species bulbs. For the most part, species bulbs are propagated, and commercial collection occurs only on a small scale. Countries that are known to export wild tulip bulbs include India (from Kashmir), Nepal, Pakistan, Iran, Iraq, and Turkey, where the genus is considered to be Rare (by IUCN). Approximately 10 percent of Holland's tulip fields are devoted to the cultivation of botanical or species tulips, mostly on the sandy soils of the northern and western parts of the country.

Because tulips have been in cultivation for centuries, it is often difficult to determine the origins of certain species. Taxonomy within *Tulipa* is quite confusing; many species have been grouped together and are regarded as synonyms. To maintain some sense of clarity, species are dealt with here as they appear in catalogs.

TULIPA (Liliaceae)

Species	Category	Notes
T. aitchisonii	W, P	Afghanistan to Kashmir (India). Wild-collected. Propagated in small quantities in the Netherlands.
T. bakeri	P	Crete. Propagated in the Netherlands. A popular cultivar, 'Lilac Wonder,' is also available.
T. batalinii	P	Uzbekistan. Propagated in small quantities in the Netherlands. Several cultivars are available: 'Bright Gem,' 'Bronze Charm.'
T. biflora	W, P	(Syn. *T. polychroma.*) Caspian and Caucasus regions, western Mediterranean. Wild-collected in Iran. Propagated in small quantities in the Netherlands. Classified by IUCN as Rare in Turkey, Endangered in Egypt, Rare in Israel and Vulnerable in Jordan.
T. chrysantha	P	Species is not known in the wild. Propagated in small quantities in the Netherlands. Listed by some authorities as T. *clusiana* var. *chrysantha.*
T. clusiana (lady tulip; candy-stick tulip)	P	Iran, Afghanistan, Iraq, Pakistan, Kashmir (India). Propagated in small quantities in the Netherlands and

		France; mostly imported to the Netherlands from Greece. Species now naturalized in some Mediterranean countries. The cultivar 'Cynthia' is grown in the Netherlands. Classified as Rare in Turkey (IUCN). Protected by law in Greece.
T. dasystemon	P	Species is possibly a synonym of *T. tarda*. According to Dutch figures, 0.7 hectares in that country are planted with *T. dasystemon* (15.4 hectares of *T. tarda* are in cultivation in the Netherlands).
T. eichleri	W, P	Transcaucasus. *T. undulatifolia* considered by some authorities to be a synonym. Wild-collected in Turkey. Propagated in the Netherlands. Classified as Rare in Ukraine (IUCN).
T. fosteriana	P	Uzbekistan. Species was formerly propagated in the Netherlands, but no longer. The source of many hybrids and cultivars, including 'Princeps' and 'Purissima'; numerous cultivars are propagated in the Netherlands.
T. gesneriana	P	Species of unknown origin; in cultivation in Turkey for centuries before being introduced to Europe in the 16th century. Widely naturalized in Europe. Most cultivars of the common tall, late-flowering tulips are derived from this species.
T. greigii	P	Turkestan, northeastern Iran. Propagated in the Netherlands. Used extensively for hybridizing; many hybrids and cultivars available. Classified as Indeterminate in the Asiatic part of its range (IUCN).

T. hageri	W, P	Greece, Asia Minor. Wild-collected in Turkey. Propagated in the Netherlands. Also available is the cultivar 'Splendens.' Some authorities view *T. hageri* as a form of *T. orphanidea.*
T. humilis	W, P	Asia Minor, north and west Iran, northern Iraq, the Caucasus. Export of wild *T. humilis* from Turkey is banned, yet bulbs continue to be exported (37,000 bulbs were exported in 1987). Some propagation in the Netherlands. Species has many variants, considered by some to be separate species (see *T. pulchella*).
T. kaufmanniana (waterlily tulip)	P	Turkestan. Propagated in the Netherlands. A key species used for hybridizing and producing cultivars.
T. kolpakowskiana	P	Turkestan. Propagated in the Netherlands.
T. kurdica	W, P	Northeastern Iraq. Wild-collected in Iraq. Propagated in small quantities in the Netherlands.
T. linifolia	P	Uzbekistan, Pamir Mountain Range. Propagated in the Netherlands. Many cultivars available. Classified as Rare (IUCN).
T. marjolettii	W, P	Eastern France. Propagated in the Netherlands.
T. maximowiczii	W	West and central Asia. Status in the wild unknown.
T. micheliana	W, P	Northeastern Iran, Turkmenistan. Possibly wild-collected in Iran. Propagated in the Netherlands. Classified as Rare in Iran (IUCN).

T. montana	W, P	(Syn. *T. wilsoniana.*) Northern Iran. Possibly wild-collected in Iran. Propagated in the Netherlands. Some authorities believe this to be a synonym of *T. wilsoniana.*
T. orphanidea	P	Greece, Crete, Bulgaria, Turkey. Propagated in the Netherlands. Also propagated is the cultivar 'Flava.' Some authorities believe *T. hageri* and *T. whittalii* are variants of *T. orphanidea.*
T. polychroma	See *T. biflora.*	
T. praecox	W, P	Southern Europe. Wild-collected in Turkey. Propagated in small quantities in the Netherlands. Widely naturalized in southern Europe. Often sold in cut flower markets in Italy. Classified as Endangered in Turkey (IUCN).
T. praestans	P	Central Asia. Propagated in the Netherlands. Many cultivars available. Classified as Vulnerable in parts of its range (IUCN).
T. pulchella	W, P	Asia Minor, Iran, the Caucasus. Propagated in the Netherlands; many cultivars available. Some authorities consider it to be a variant of *T. humulis.* Listings in catalogs often retain the earlier nomenclature of *T. pulchella humulis* and *T. pulchella violacea.*
T. saxatilis	W, P	Crete, possibly southwestern Turkey. Some propagation in the Netherlands. May be subject to specialist collection. The taxonomy of this species is confusing; thought by some to be a synonym of *T. bakeri.* Protected by law in Greece. Classified as Rare in Turkey (IUCN).
T. sylvestris	P	Europe, Iran, northern Africa. Widely naturalized in Europe. Propagated in the Netherlands.

T. tarda	P	Turkestan. Extensive propagation in the Netherlands. Species reproduces rapidly by means of stolons; easy to cultivate. Some authorities believe this species to be a synonym of *T. dasystemon*. Classified as Rare (IUCN).
T. tubergeniana	P	Central Asia. Propagated in the Netherlands; many cultivars available including 'Keukenhof.'
T. turkestanica	P	Turkestan, Central Asia, northwestern China. Some propagation in the Netherlands.
T. undulatifolia	W, P	Transcaucasus. Restricted distribution. Wild-collected in Turkey. Propagated in the Netherlands. Considered by some authorities to be a synonym of *T. eichleri*. Classified as Vulnerable in Greece (IUCN).
T. urumiensis	P	Northwestern Iran. Propagated in the Netherlands.
T. vvedenskyi	P	Central Asia. Propagated in the Netherlands. Cultivars available including 'Tangerine Bleu.' Classified as Rare (IUCN).
T. whittallii	P	Turkey. Propagated in the Netherlands. Some authorities consider this species to be a variant of *T. hageri*.
T. wilsoniana	See *T. montana*.	

URGINEA

The genus *Urginea*, known as the sea onion or sea squill, consists of approximately 30 species distributed from the Mediterranean to South Africa. Although few species of *Urginea* are considered worth cultivating, the genus is well known among indigenous peoples for its medicinal qualities. It is poisonous to cattle and has been used as a rat poison.

The species that occurs most often in trade is the sea onion (*U. maritima*), a species that prefers sandy soil. As a result, it does not always fare well in the garden, which usually has rich soil. In addition, it does not tolerate frost.

URGINEA (Liliaceae)

Species	Category	Notes
U. maritima (sea onion; sea squill)	W, P	Mediterranean Europe, northern Africa, Middle East. Wild-collected in Portugal. Propagated in the United States.

ZEPHYRANTHES

Zephyranthes is a small genus of approximately 30 species distributed from the southeastern United States through Central America and the Caribbean down to Argentina. Species in this genus are commonly known as zephyr lilies. These lilies prefer a moist environment, and temperatures ideally should never drop below 20°F.

Propagation of *Zephyranthes* is best achieved by offsets, although the plants set seed freely. Numerous growers are propagating species of *Zephyranthes*; it is not known to what degree members of the genus are wild-collected.

ZEPHYRANTHES (Amaryllidaceae)

Genus, Species	Category	Notes
Z. atamasco (Atamasco lily; swamp lily)	W, P	(Syn. *Amaryllis atamasco.*) Maryland south to Florida. Wild-collected in the United States. Propagated by division in the United States. Maryland: Highly Rare.

Z. candida	P	(Syn. *Amaryllis candida.*) South America. Propagated by division in the United States and on a small scale in the Netherlands. Exported from India.
Z. citrina	P	(Syn. *Z. eggersoniana.*) Guyana and Trinidad. Propagated by division in the United States; also propagated in the Netherlands.
Z. grandiflora (fairy lily)	P	(Syn. *Z. carinata, Z. tsouii.*) Guatemala. Naturalized in many warm countries, including South Africa. Propagated by division in the United States; propagated in the Netherlands.
Z. rosea	P	Guatemala, West Indies. Propagated by division in the United States; propagated in the Netherlands. Exported from India.

VII.

Insectivorous Plants

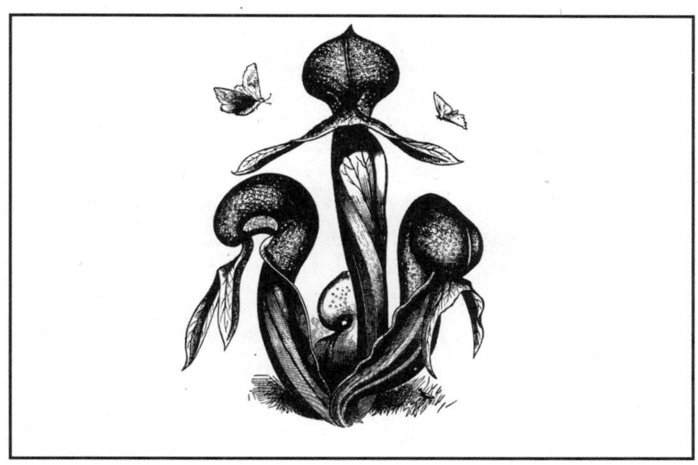

The carnivores are some of the world's most fascinating and intriguing plants. Although the best-known example is North America's Venus flytrap, carnivorous plants comprise 15 genera with over 500 species, each of which has evolved its own specialized method of trapping insects and other prey. Most carnivorous plant species occur in mineral-deficient ecosystems, where they cannot derive sufficient nutrients from the soil alone. In the United States, carnivorous plants are often found in acidic soils low in nitrogen, such as peat bogs or coastal plains.

While most other plants have substantial root systems that absorb essential nutrients, carnivorous plants have roots that are often insufficient to utilize fully the minerals existing in their environment. To supplement their nutrient absorption capacity, carnivorous plants "trap" and digest unsuspecting prey, including insects and small animals.

Two types of trapping mechanisms, active and passive, are found among species of carnivorous plants. Active traps found in Venus flytraps (*Dionaea*), bladderworts (*Utricularia*), sundews (*Drosera*), and butterworts (*Pinguicula*) use rapid motion to capture prey, with plant parts closing down into a cagelike structure. The sundews and butterworts also have an interior adhesive substance that further hinders escape. Passive traps are seen in species such as the pitcher plants (*Sarracenia* and *Nepenthes*) and cobra plants (*Darlingtonia*). These traps use ingenious structural designs to entrap prey and make escape impossible. After capture, the plant secretes acids and enzymes to digest its prey.

In recent decades, carnivorous plant habitat has decreased significantly. In the southeastern United States especially, shrubs and trees have overgrown much of the open, sunny bog habitat prefered by sundews, pitcher plants, and Venus flytraps. Previously, periodic surface fires contributed to these bogs' lifespans by burning down competing vegetation. Today, however, fire prevention to protect newly expanded urban areas enables young woody plants to take root and eventually overtake and replace the wetland habitat needed to support carnivorous plant species. In addition, land clearance for development and forestry activities has been devastating for carnivorous plants. With the creation of pine plantations in the south, bogs have been filled in or drained. Habitat loss is accelerating, with many wetland plant populations decreasing and even disappearing from some areas.

Carnivorous plants have also fallen prey to the excesses of the horticultural trade. These unusual plants have been admired and cultivated for centuries, but recent overcollection of wild specimens is causing severe problems for some populations. Although most species are easy to cultivate, the time required to produce plants of salable size, as well as the equipment expense, leads many commercial traders to collect plants from the wild instead of propagating them. The most common species in trade are the pitcher plants and the Venus flytrap. One pitcher plant whose population has been severely depleted by overcollection and commercial trade is the giant tropical pitcher plant or king monkey cup (*Nepenthes rajah*), from Mt. Kinabalu in Borneo, a plant famous for having the largest pitchers in the genus. Some of these extraordinary cups reach 13 inches in length and 6 inches in width, large enough to trap and digest small animals.

North American pitcher plants are harvested for the floriculture industry. Attractive and unusual, the long green pitchers are cut and sold for floral arrangements. Most of these pitchers are used within the United States, although some are exported to Europe and Asia. Virtually all of the pitchers available in florist's shops in the United States are of wild origin. While efforts are under way to learn how to manage pitcher plant populations for sustainable harvest, these efforts are still experimental. At present, it is unknown what effect, if any, the removal of a trap has on a plant. Some scientists speculate that the removal of the plants' nutrient source may cause undue stress; also, the walking around associated with collection may cause soil compaction damaging to the fragile bog ecosystems.

Several carnivorous plants are protected under the U.S. Endangered Species Act. Three North American pitcher plants, the mountain sweet pitcher plant (*Sarracenia jonesii*), the Alabama canebrake pitcher plant (*Sarracenia alabamensis* ssp. *alabamensis*), and the green pitcher plant (*Sarracenia oreophila*), are listed as Endangered. It is therefore illegal to sell these species through interstate commerce or to export them.

Some species are also protected under the Convention on International Trade in Endangered Species of Wild Fauna and Flora (CITES). Trade in all North American pitcher plants, tropical pitcher plants (*Nepenthes*), the California pitcher plant (*Darlingtonia californica*), the Western Australian pitcher plant (*Cephalotus follicularis*), and the Venus flytrap is regulated under CITES.

The Venus flytrap, native only to the coastal plain of South and North Carolina, was afforded protection in Appendix II of CITES as recently as 1992. Conservationists are alarmed at the quantity of Venus flytraps sold in the United States as novelty plants, primarily because this species is still collected from the wild. In many cases, the flytraps are collected, often illegally, by people who are supplementing meager incomes. In 1990, over 1.1 million Venus flytraps were exported overseas from North Carolina; it is estimated that this quantity included over 300,000 wild specimens. Of these exports, 70 percent went to the Netherlands, with Germany, Japan, and the United Kingdom importing most of the remainder. Although there are no definitive data on the number of plants sold within the United States, in 1981 the quantity was estimated to be between 1.4 and 4.5 million plants.

Both South Carolina and North Carolina have laws in place to protect the Venus flytrap. In fact, in 1991 North Carolina elevated the plant to the status of Special Concern. Under this listing, Venus flytraps cannot be collected without the permission of the landowner. The permission must be written, and dated, and is valid for not more than 180 days. It is illegal to sell unlawfully collected Venus flytraps. Fines of $100 to $500 can be levied for a first offense, and $500 to $1,000 for a subsequent offense. As before, it is illegal to collect flytraps on public lands.

With regard to propagation, *Drosera*, the sundew, is easy to propagate from seed and even easier from cuttings; some species grow to flowering size in one season, enabling growers to amass a sizable stock without much difficulty. *Sarracenia* is also easy to propagate by seed; yet the time involved has inhibited development of commercial propagation operations. The fastest-growing North American pitcher plant is *S. rubra*, which can grow from seed to flowering size in two to three years. Four years are required for the other species of *Sarracenia*. The Venus flytrap can be propagated by division and by seed; yet, like the other carnivorous plants, it is collected from natural areas because it is less expensive to collect than to propagate.

INSECTIVOROUS PLANTS

Genus, Species	Category	Notes
DARLINGTONIA (Sarraceniaceae)		
D. californica (cobra lily; California pitcher plant)	W, P	Northern California, southwestern Oregon. Both wild-collected and propagated by seed in the United States. Oregon: of Concern. Listed in Appendix II of CITES.

DIONAEA (Droseraceae)		
D. muscipula (Venus flytrap)	W, P	Coastal plain of North and South Carolina. Collection is prohibited in South Carolina. Wild-collected in North Carolina. Propagated in small quantities in United Kingdom, and in large quantities in the Netherlands; one nursery produces several hundred thousand plants each year. In the United States, propagation is by tissue culture, division, seed, and leaf base and leaf blade culture. Large bulbs are likely to be of wild origin. North Carolina: protected and listed as Special Concern. South Carolina: protected and classified as Critically Imperiled; Of Concern. Listed in Appendix II of CITES.
DROSERA (Droseraceae)		
D. adelae (sundew)	P	Queensland, Australia. Propagated in the United States. Propagation from seed and leaf cuttings. Possibly wild-collected in Australia.
D. beleziana	—	Not a recognized species.
D. binata (fork-leaved sundew)	P	Eastern Australia, New Zealand, Tasmania. Several varieties and forms exist; most are native to temperate areas, some to tropical zones. Propagated by seed and leaf cuttings in the United States and Europe. Possibly wild-collected in Australia.
D. burmannii (sundew)	P	India to Japan, Australia. A short-lived species. Propagated by seed and tissue culture. Possibly wild-collected in Australia.

D. capensis (Cape sundew)	P	South Africa. Propagated by seed and by leaf and root cuttings in the United States and Europe.
D. capillaris (pink sundew)	W, P	Coastal plain of southeastern Virginia south to Florida and west to Texas; also found in the West Indies, Mexico, south to northern South America. A short-lived species. Propagated by seed and leaf cuttings. Maryland: protected and listed as Endangered. Tennessee: Threatened.
D. communis	—	Not a recognized species.
D. dichotoma	—	Variety of *D. binata*.
D. filiformis (thread-leaf sundew)	W, P	There are two varieties of this species. *D. filiformis* var. *filiformis* occurs from Cape Cod along the coastal plain south to South Carolina; leaf blades grow to 25cm and have reddish glands. *D. filiformis* var. *tracyi* occurs from South Carolina to northern Florida and Louisiana; leaves reach 50 cm and are green, making it the largest variety of *Drosera*. Propagated by seed or leaf cuttings in the United States. Connecticut: Endangered. Rhode Island: protected and listed as Endangered.
D. hamiltonii (sundew)	P	Western Australia. Relatively difficult to propagate. Possibly wild-collected.
D. indica	—	Not a recognized species.
D. intermedia (spathulate-leaved sundew; spoon-leaved sundew)	P	Europe, Asia, eastern North America, West Indies, northern South America. Propagated by seed and division. Florida: protected and listed as Threatened; Rare (TNC) . Illinois: protected and listed as Threatened. Indiana: Rare. Kentucky: Endangered.

		Louisiana: Critically Imperiled. Ohio: protected and listed as Endangered. Virginia: Rare (TNC).
D. prolifera	—	Not a recognized species.
D. rotundifolia (round-leaved sundew)	W, P	Northern and Southern Hemisphere. Used in traditional medicine in Europe. Propagated by seed or leaf cuttings. Colorado: Rare. Delaware: Imperiled. Illinois: protected and listed as Endangered. Iowa: protected and listed as Endangered. Ohio: Potentially Threatened.
D. spathulata (spoon-leaf sundew)	P	Australia, Tasmania, New Zealand, China, Japan, Hong Kong, Malaysia, the Philippines. Propagated by seed and leaf cuttings. Possibly wild-collected in Australia.
D. tracyi	See *D. filiformis*.	
PINGUICULA (Lentibulariaceae)		
P. caerulea (violet butterwort)	W, P	Southeastern coastal plain from North Carolina to central Florida. Propagated by seed and leaf cuttings.
P. ionantha (violet-flowered butterwort)	W, P	Florida panhandle. Florida: protected and listed as Endangered; Imperiled.
P. lutea (yellow butterwort)	W, P	Southeastern coastal plain from North Carolina to Louisiana. Propagated by seed and leaf cuttings. Louisiana: Imperiled.
P. planifolia (Chapman's butterwort)	W, P	Florida panhandle west to Louisiana. Propagated by seed and leaf cuttings. Alabama: Imperiled. Florida: protected and listed as Endangered; Imperiled. Mississippi: Imperiled.

P. primuliflora (southern butterwort)	W, P	Coastal plain from northern Florida west to Mississippi. Propagated by leaf cuttings or by plantlets that sprout out from the end of the older leaves. Mississippi: Rare (TNC).
P. pumila (dwarf butterwort)	W, P	Southeastern coastal plain from North Carolina to Texas. Alabama: Critically Imperiled. Oklahoma: Critically Imperiled.
SARRACENIA (Sarraceniaceae)		
S. alata (pale pitcher plant)	W	Gulf coastal plain from southern Alabama to eastern Texas. Pitchers harvested for the floriculture industry. Listed in Appendix II of CITES.
S. flava (yellow pitcher plant)	W, P	Southeastern United States from Virginia to Florida panhandle. Propagated in the Netherlands. Pitchers harvested for the floriculture industry. Primarily wild-collected in the United States. Georgia: protected and listed as Threatened. Virginia: Imperiled. Listed in Appendix II of CITES.
S. leucophylla (white-topped pitcher plant)	W, P	Southwestern Georgia to western Florida panhandle. Propagated in the Netherlands. Pitchers are harvested for the floriculture industry. Primarily wild-collected in the United States. Florida: protected and listed as Endangered; (Rare TNC). Georgia: protected and listed as Threatened. Mississippi: Rare (TNC). Listed in Appendix II of CITES.
S. minor (hooded pitcher plant)	W, P	Southeastern coastal plain from southern North Carolina to Florida panhandle. Primarily wild-collected. Propagated in the Netherlands. Georgia: protected and listed as Threatened. Listed in Appendix II of CITES.

S. psittacina (parrot pitcher plant)	W, P	Southeastern coastal plain from Georgia to Southern Mississippi. Propagated in the Netherlands. Primarily wild-collected. Georgia: protected and listed as Threatened. Louisiana: Rare (TNC). Listed in Appendix II of CITES.
S. purpurea (northern pitcher plant)	W, P	Canada, eastern United States. Propagated in the Netherlands. Primarily wild-collected in the United States. Alabama: Rare (TNC). Georgia: protected and listed as Endangered. Illinois: protected and listed as Endangered. Maryland: protected and listed as Threatened. Michigan: *S. purpurea* forma *heterophylla* is protected and listed as Threatened. Mississippi: Critically Imperiled. New Hampshire: protected and listed as Special Concern. Ohio: protected and listed as Threatened. Virginia: Critically Imperiled. Listed in Appendix II of CITES.
S. rubra (sweet pitcher plant)	W	Southeastern coastal plain from southern North Carolina to southwestern Alabama and northern Florida. Alabama: *S. rubra* ssp. *alabamensis* is listed as Critically Imperiled; *S. rubra* ssp. *wherryi* is listed as Rare (TNC). Florida: protected and listed as Endangered; Imperiled. Georgia: protected and listed as Endangered. Illinois: protected and listed as Endangered. Mississippi: *S. rubra* spp. *wherryi* is listed as Critically Imperiled. South Carolina: Critically Imperiled. *S. rubra* ssp. *jonesii* (syn. *S. jonesii*) and *S. rubra* ssp. *alabamensis* (syn. *S. alabamensis* ssp. *alabamensis*) are listed as federally Endangered; both are listed in Appendix I of CITES.

VIII.

Terrestrial Orchids

The Orchidaceae is the largest family of flowering plants in the world, comprising over 25,000 species. The greatest concentration and diversity of orchid species occurs in the tropics, but orchids are present on every continent except Antarctica.

Orchid growth form varies significantly. In the tropics, most are epiphytes, plants that grow perched on trees, rocks, or other above-ground surfaces. Instead of deriving nourishment through their roots from the soil as do their terrestrial counterparts, epiphytes absorb nutrients from rainwater, air, and organic debris. By contrast, orchids native to the temperate zones are largely terrestrial. These species are rooted in the soil and take in nutrients by means of a system of fine root hairs.

The history of the trade in orchids is particularly instructive. These diverse plants were collected in huge quantities in the second half of the 19th century to support a growing European fancy. England's flourishing nursery industry hired countless plant collectors to travel the world in search of new orchid species. Profits were so spectacular that competition between collectors for new and intriguing species quickly escalated out of control. When new orchids were introduced on the market, collectors often supplied false locations of origin to throw their rivals off track. Every effort was made to bring back as many plants as possible, and sometimes remaining plants were destroyed to ensure that a collection would be unique. In one instance, approximately 4,000 trees were felled in Colombia to acquire 10,000 specimens of the delicate orchid *Odontoglossum crispum*, now extremely rare in the wild.

Today, the vast majority of tropical orchids in trade are grown in greenhouses around the world. Hybrids, selections, and cultivars make up the bulk of the trade. Horticulturists have been able to create stunning colors and patterns by crossing species not only within a genus but also between genera. As a result, the demand for wild specimens has decreased significantly.

Nevertheless, a market still exists for wild orchid plants. The World Conservation Union (IUCN) has studied the status of orchids worldwide and has determined, in an examination of 3,828 species, that 906 are "threatened." However, the status of the majority of species in the wild remains unclear. When species are known to be threatened, that status is not necessarily the result of overcollection; habitat destruction has been the most devastating factor contributing to the decline of orchids worldwide. Compounding this loss, desirable orchid species are ruthlessly sought after at ever more remote localities for international trade.

Trade within the United States of orchid species native to North America appears to be concentrated in the lady slipper orchids (*Cypripedium* spp.) Most species in this genus are very difficult, perhaps nearly impossible, to propagate artificially. Fortunately, some recent efforts to propagate several *Cypripedium*, especially showy ladyslipper (*C. reginae*) and yellow ladyslipper (*C. calceolus*), from laboratory-germinated seed have been successful. Laboratory-grown seedlings of these two species are now available for purchase. Buyers should be aware, however, that mature plants in this genus are primarily wild-collected. The only species for which propagated mature specimens are available is *C. calceolus*, but even with this species, most plants are of wild origin.

Several other genera of terrestrial orchids are

popular in American gardens. *Bletilla*, which occurs in eastern Asia, Taiwan, and the adjacent islands, is a showy genus consisting of nine species. Hyacinth orchid (*B. striata*) is the most heavily traded species in the genus; over 145,000 plants were traded internationally in 1989. Although this species is propagated to some extent in Japan, commercial collection continues to pose a threat. *Bletilla striata* is classified by IUCN as Threatened throughout Japan and Endangered or Vulnerable in some specific locations.

Pleione, the window-sill orchid, is also traded in significant quantities. The most heavily traded species is *Pleione formosana*; in 1989, approximately 212,000 of these plants appeared in international trade. This species occurs in Taiwan and possibly in eastern China. In the past, it was collected extensively for export; now it is propagated in Taiwan, as are many spectacular hybrids. Other species of *Pleione* are also traded, many of them wild-collected in China, Nepal, and other Asian countries.

The following list consists of North American species, as well as a few species that occur in Europe and Asia. Gardeners should be particularly careful with regard to North American native species: although some can be propagated artificially, the vast majority are collected from the wild. If a plant is advertised as propagated, the consumer should question the grower or vendor. Gardeners are encouraged to buy propagated orchids; propagators need support, and wild populations would benefit from a reduction in collecting pressure.

TERRESTRIAL ORCHIDS

Genus, Species	Category	Notes
AMERORCHIS		
A. rotundifolia (small round-leaved orchis)	W	Northern North America, including Montana, Wisconsin, Michigan, and New York. Maine: Threatened. New York: protected and listed as Vulnerable. Michigan: protected and listed as Endangered. Wisconsin: protected and listed as Threatened. Listed in Appendix II of CITES.

APLECTRUM

A. hyemale (puttyroot)	W	Eastern United States. Wild-collected, although propagation is possible by division. In the past puttyroot tubers were collected for medicinal purposes. Alabama: Critically Imperiled. Connecticut: Special Concern; Extirpated. Delaware: Critically Imperiled. Massachusetts: protected and listed as Endangered. Mississippi: Critically Imperiled. New Jersey: Endangered; Critically Imperiled. New York: protected and listed as Vulnerable; Critically Imperiled. Oklahoma: Pennsylvania: Rare (TNC). Critically Imperiled. Vermont: protected and listed as Threatened. Listed in Appendix II of CITES.

BLETILLA

B. striata (hyacinth orchid)	W, P	Japan, China, eastern Tibet, Okinawa. Propagated in Japan; wild-collected throughout its range. Sometimes marketed as *Bletilla hyacinthina*. Classified as Indeterminate in Japan (IUCN). Listed in Appendix II of CITES.

CALYPSO

C. bulbosa (calypso; fairy slipper)	W	Scandinavia to Japan; northern North America from southern Alaska to Newfoundland; also in Great Lakes region and high elevations of Utah, Arizona, New Mexico. Extremely difficult to cultivate following transplant. Threatened in Japan by overcollection. Maine: Rare. Michigan: protected and listed as Threatened. New Hampshire: protected and listed as Endangered. New York: protected and listed as Vulnerable. South Dakota: Rare. Vermont: protected and listed as Threatened. Wisconsin: protected and listed as Threatened. Listed in Appendix II of CITES.

CYPRIPEDIUM

C. acaule (pink ladyslipper; moccasin flower)	W	Eastern North America. No nursery is propagating this species on a commercial scale. Wild-collected for both the horticultural and medicinal trade. Wild plants are particularly vulnerable when transplanted because of extensive root systems that are very sensitive and easily bruised. Alabama: Rare (TNC). Georgia: protected and listed as Special Concern. Illinois: protected and listed as Endangered. New Hampshire: protected and listed as Special Concern. Tennessee: protected and listed as Endangered. Listed in Appendix II of CITES.
C. calceolus (yellow ladyslipper)	W, P	Asia, Europe and eastern North America from Newfoundland south to Tennessee. Primarily wild-collected; some propagation taking place by division. If transplanted, said to be fairly easy to cultivate as this species is robust and able to survive in a variety of soil conditions. *C. calceolus* is classified by IUCN as Endangered in Japan; Indeterminate throughout Europe; almost Extinct in the United Kingdom. Georgia: protected and listed as Special Concern. Oklahoma: Imperiled. Listed in Appendix II of CITES.
C. calceolus var. *parviflorum* (small ladyslipper)	W, P	Northern United States, Canada. Some propagation taking place (extremely limited). Colorado: Rare. Ohio: protected and listed as Threatened. Oregon: Extirpated. Idaho: Endangered; Critically Imperiled. Illinois: protected and listed as Endangered. Indiana: Kentucky: Endangered. Massachusetts: protected and listed as Endangered. Montana: Sensitive; Imperiled. New Hampshire: protected and listed as Endangered.

		North Dakota: Threatened. Pennsylvania: protected and listed as Endangered. Rhode Island: Threatened. Washington: Endangered. Wyoming: Rare (TNC). Listed in Appendix II of CITES.
C. calceolus var. *pubescens* (large yellow ladyslipper)	W, P	Quebec and Newfoundland, south to Georgia, Alabama, and Texas. Some propagation taking place (extremely limited). Alabama: Rare (TNC). Mississippi: Imperiled. Ohio: Potentially Endangered. New Hampshire: protected and listed as Threatened. New Mexico: protected and listed as Endangered. Rhode Island: Threatened. Wyoming: Critically Imperiled. Listed in Appendix II of CITES.
C. pubescens	See *C. calceolus* var. *pubescens.*	
C. reginae (showy ladyslipper)	W	Eastern North America from Tennessee to Newfoundland. Wild-collected; propagation is possible by division. One U.S. nursery is now propagating this species from seed in the laboratory; their plants are sold as seedlings only. Arkansas: Endangered. Connecticut: Endangered. Illinois: protected and listed as Endangered. Iowa: protected and listed as Endangered. Kentucky: Endangered. Maine: Special Concern. Maryland: protected and listed as Endangered; Extirpated. Massachusetts: protected and listed as Special Concern. New Hampshire: protected and listed as Endangered. Ohio: protected and listed as Threatened. Pennsylvania: protected and listed as Threatened. New Jersey: Endangered; Critically Imperiled. Tennessee: protected and listed as Endangered. Virginia: Critically Imperiled. Listed in Appendix II of CITES.

EPIPACTIS		
E. gigantea (giant helleborine)	W, P	Southern British Columbia to California, Arizona, New Mexico. Primarily wild-collected; some propagation by division at several nurseries. Colorado: Rare. Idaho: Rare (TNC). Montana: Threatened; Critically Imperiled. New Mexico: protected and listed as Endangered. Oklahoma: Critically Imperiled. South Dakota: Critically Rare. Washington: Sensitive. Wyoming: Critically Imperiled. Listed in Appendix II of CITES.
GALEARIS		
G. spectabilis (showy orchis)	W	(Syn. *Orchis spectabilis.*) Quebec south to Alabama, and west through central and Great Lakes states. Primarily wild-collected, although not impossible to propagate. Alabama: Rare (TNC). Maine: Threatened. Michigan: Special Concern. Mississippi: Critically Imperiled. New Hampshire: protected and listed as Threatened. Rhode Island: protected and listed as Endangered. Listed in Appendix II of CITES.
GOODYERA		
G. oblongifolia (Menzies' rattlesnake plantain; giant rattlesnake plantain)	W, P	Western North America; also in New Brunswick, Maine, south central states, and Arizona. Primarily wild-collected; also propagated by several specialty growers. Maine: Endangered. Listed in Appendix II of CITES.
G. pubescens (downy rattlesnake plantain)	W, P	Northeastern United States to Alabama. Primarily wild-collected; some propagation. Florida: protected and listed as Threatened; Imperiled. Maine: Rare. Mississippi: Critically Imperiled. Listed in Appendix II of CITES.

G. tesselata (tesselated rattlesnake plantain; checkered rattlesnake plantain)	W, P	Northeastern North America from Newfoundland to northern Virginia. Primarily wild-collected; some propagation may occur. Maryland: protected and listed as Endangered; Extirpated. New Jersey: Endangered; Critically Imperiled. Ohio: Presumed Extirpated. Pennsylvania: Imperiled. Listed in Appendix II of CITES.
HABENARIA		
H. blephariglottis	See *Platanthera blephariglottis.*	
H. ciliaris	See *Platanthera ciliaris.*	
H. fimbrata	See *Platanthera grandiflora.*	
H. psycodes	See *Platanthera psycodes.*	
LIPARIS		
L. lilifolia (mauve sleekwort; purple twayblade)	W, P	Northeastern United States, and Minnesota south to Mississippi, Alabama, and Georgia. Primarily wild-collected; some propagation may occur. Connecticut: Endangered. Delaware: Imperiled. Oklahoma: Critically Imperiled. Michigan: Special Concern. New York: protected and listed as Rare; Critically Imperiled. Rhode Island: Threatened. Vermont: protected and listed as Threatened. Listed in Appendix II of CITES.
ORCHIS		
O. spectabilis	See *Galearis spectabilis.*	
PLATANTHERA		
P. blephariglottis (white finged orchid)	W	(Syn. *Habenaria blephariglottis.*) Newfoundland west to Michigan, northeastern United States. Connecticut: Endangered. Delaware: Critically

		Imperiled. Louisiana: Critically Imperiled. Maryland: protected and listed as Threatened. Mississippi: Imperiled. Ohio: protected and listed as Endangered. New Hampshire: protected and listed as Special Concern. Rhode Island: Threatened. Virginia: Imperiled. Listed in Appendix II of CITES.
P. ciliaris (yellow fringed orchid)	W	(Syn. *Habenaria ciliaris.*) Eastern United States and southeastern Canada. Wild-collected in the United States. Connecticut: Threatened. Illinois: protected and listed as Endangered. Indiana: protected and listed as Endangered. Maryland: protected and listed as Threatened. Michigan: protected and listed as Threatened. Missouri: Endangered. New Jersey: Imperiled. New York: protected and listed as Threatened; Critically Imperiled. Ohio: protected and listed as Threatened. Oklahoma: Critically Imperiled. Rhode Island: protected and listed as Endangered. Listed in Appendix II of CITES.
P. grandiflora (large purple fringed orchid)	W	(Syn. *Habenaria fimbrata.*) Northeastern North America from Newfoundland south to North Carolina and west to Wisconsin. Wild-collected in the United States. Delaware: Extirpated. Maryland: protected and listed as Threatened. New Hampshire: protected and listed as Special Concern. New Jersey: Rare (TNC). Ohio: Presumed Extirpated. Tennessee: protected and listed as Endangered. Virginia: Critically Imperiled. Listed in Appendix II of CITES.
P. psycodes (lesser purple fringe orchid)	W	(Syn. *Habenaria psycodes.*) Southeastern United States. Illinois: protected and listed as Endangered. Indiana: Rare. Iowa: protected and listed as Endangered. Kentucky: Endangered.

		Maryland: protected and listed as Endangered; Possibly Extirpated. Ohio: protected and listed as Endangered. Tennessee: Threatened. West Virginia: Critically Imperiled. Listed in Appendix II of CITES.
PLEIONE		
P. formosana (window-sill orchid)	P	Taiwan, possibly China. Formerly wild-collected; now propagated in Taiwan. Protected in Taiwan. Listed in Appendix II of CITES.
P. forrestii	W, P	China, northern Myanmar. Wild-collected in China. Only member of the genus with yellow flowers; used extensively in plant breeding; many hybrids are available. Listed in Appendix II of CITES.
SPIRANTHES		
S. cernua (nodding ladies' tresses)	W	Central and eastern North America Wild-collected in the United States. Propagation by division is possible. Delaware: Rare (TNC). Oklahoma: *S. cernua* var. *odorata* is listed as Critically Imperiled. South Dakota: Rare. Listed in Appendix II of CITES.
TIPULARIA		
T. discolor (crane-fly orchid)	W, P	Eastern United States. Primarily wild-collected; propagated on a minor scale. Propagation impossible from seed and very slow by division. Massachusetts: protected and listed as Endangered. Michigan: protected and listed as Threatened. Missouri: Endangered. New York: protected and listed as Threatened; Critically Imperiled. Oklahoma: Critically Imperiled. Pennsylvania: Imperiled. Listed in Appendix II of CITES.

Sources of Information

American Horticultural Society
P.O. Box 0105
Mount Vernon, VA 22121

Nursery Sources for Propagated Native Plants contains lists of mail-order nurseries selling propagated plants or seed collected in a responsible manner.

American Rock Garden Society Seed Exchange
Carole Wilder, Director
221 W. 9th Street
Hastings, MN 55033

A seedlist has been prepared by the Minnesota Chapter of the ARGS.

Andersen Horticultural Library
Minnesota Landscape Arboretum
3675 Arboretum Drive, Box 39
Chanhassen, MN 55317

The *Andersen Horticultural Library's Source List of Plants and Seeds* is available for $29.95; this publication contains over 1,200 listings of seed and nursery catalogs. Although an effort has been made to exclude nurseries that sell wild-collected plants, gardeners should query nurseries to be certain that the plants are indeed propagated. For example, numerous sources are listed for the pink ladyslipper, although experts agree that no one is propagating this species on a commercial scale.

Center for Plant Conservation
Missouri Botanical Garden
P.O. Box 299
St. Louis, MO 63166

This organization can provide information about endangered species and the conservation status of native plants. For $15.00 in 1992, the annually published *Plant Conservation Directory* contains names and addresses of state wildlife agencies (including Natural Heritage Programs that distribute lists of endangered species) and briefly summarizes any legislation pertaining to plant protection.

Eastern Native Plant Alliance
P.O. Box 6101
McLean, VA 22106

This alliance includes botanical gardens and arboretums, native plant societies, nurseries, conservation organizations, and numerous others who work together to stimulate conservation efforts to protect native plants. A quarterly newsletter is produced, and there are annual meetings.

Gardening By Mail 2.
1988. Barbara J. Barton.
Tusker Press
Sebastopol, California

Many bookstores carry this directory of mail-order nurseries and garden suppliers. A very useful reference tool, it also contains addresses of professional and native plant societies, libraries, magazines, and horticultural books. One caution: the nursery listings are general and do not distinguish between operations selling propagated plants and those selling wild-collected ones.

Hortus Northwest
P.O. Box 955
Canby, OR 97013

A Pacific Northwest Native Plant Directory is produced and updated periodically. This publication is an extensive listing of commercial sources of Northwest natives. There is no disclaimer indicating that nurseries sell only propagated plants.

Native Plant Societies

Consult the native plant society in your state. Many have listings of nurseries that propagate plants or that have seed available for exchange or purchase.

New England Wild Flower Society
Garden in the Woods
180 Hemenway Road
Framingham, MA 01701

The society conducts research on propagation of native species and also produces *Nursery Sources: Native Plants and Wildflowers,* which is available for $4.95. This publication only lists nurseries that offer propagated plants. Also available is the latest edition of the *Seed and Book Catalog,* which lists seed of 250 native plants. Contact this society for the most up-to-date information on propagation and sources of propagated native plants.

North Carolina Botanical Garden
Box 3375 Totten Center
University of North Carolina
Chapel Hill, NC 27514

A list of *Propagated Plant and Seed Sources for Southeastern Native Plants* is available.

Soil and Water Conservation Society
7515 Northeast Ankeny Road
Ankeny, Iowa 50021

This organization produces *Sources of Native Seeds and Plants*, which is available for $3.00. The publication lists sources of native species, both wild-collected and propagated, but does not provide any information about whether the nurseries propagate or collect.

The Theodore Payne Foundation
10459 Tuxford Street
Sun Valley, California 91352

This organization produces a listing of California native seed suppliers.

This brief list represents a starting point from which to begin the search for propagated plants. It is important to remember that, if there is no definitive statement about a plant's origin, question the vendor. Lists of sources of native plants are not necessarily lists of propagated plants. Responsibility for each purchase rests on the shoulders of the gardener.

GLOSSARY

Bulb. A modified leaf bud consisting of an underground stem and leaf bases. Serves as a storage organ.

CITES. The Convention on International Trade in Endangered Species of Wild Fauna and Flora, the world's largest wildlife conservation agreement. As of November 1992, 117 nations were parties to this treaty.

Cultivar. A plant variety that has originated in and been maintained in cultivation. Cultivars do not occur in the wild and are not botanical species; they are always propagated.

Critically Imperiled. The Nature Conservancy (TNC) has developed a system for ranking the conservation status of species on both global and state levels. For the purposes of this guide, only state listings are recorded. The state category reflecting the most significant threat is "S1," which is defined as "extremely rare and *critically imperiled* with five or fewer occurrences." Use of TNC terminology is widespread; many organizations and individuals are familiar with the categories.

Division. Propagation by separating a plant into two or more pieces. Each piece must have roots and a bud.

Hybrid. A plant resulting from the crossing of two different species or subspecies.

Imperiled. The Nature Conservancy (TNC) has developed a system for ranking the conservation status of species on both global and state levels. For the purposes of this guide, only state listings are recorded. The state category "S2" is defined as "very rare and *imperiled* with 6 to 20 occurrences in the state." Use of TNC terminology is widespread; many organizations and individuals are familiar with the categories.

Indeterminate. The World Conservation Union (also known as the International Union for Conservation of Nature and Natural Resources or IUCN) has developed a system for ranking the conservation status of species. "Indeterminate" is defined as "taxa known to be either Extinct, Endangered, Vulnerable, or Rare, but for which there is insufficient information to determine which category is most appropriate."

IUCN conservation categories. The World Conservation Union (also known as the International Union for Conservation of Nature and Natural Resources or IUCN) has developed a system for ranking the conservation status of species. The categories are: extinct, endangered, vulnerable, rare, indeterminate, and not threatened.

Not Threatened. The World Conservation Union (also known as the International Union for Conservation of Nature and Natural Resources or IUCN) has developed a system for ranking the conservation status of species. Species that are considered to be neither rare nor threatened are described in this guide as "Not Threatened."

Nursery Grown. A confusing term occasionally used by growers and plant vendors. This term implies that a plant labeled as such is propagated; however, sometimes the term is used for plants that have been transplanted from the wild and allowed to increase in size in the nursery. Thus, the term is ambiguous; gardeners should request clarification from the grower or vendor to determine its exact meaning.

Offset. A lateral shoot arising from the base of the plant, ending in a bud.

Rare (IUCN). The World Conservation Union (also known as the International Union for Conservation of Nature and Natural Resources or IUCN) has developed a system for ranking the conservation status of species. "Rare" is defined as "taxa with small global populations that are not considered to be endangered or vulnerable, but that are at risk."

Rare (TNC). The Nature Conservancy (TNC) has developed a system for ranking the conservation status of species on both global and state levels. For the purposes of this guide, only state listings are recorded. The state category "S3" is defined as "*rare* to uncommon with between 20 to 100 occurrences."

Rhizome. A horizontal stem that produces leaves or stems at the apex. Rhizomes are often found underground and may be enlarged due to food storage activity.

Vulnerable. The World Conservation Union (also known as the International Union for the Conservation of Nature and Natural Resources or IUCN) has developed a system for ranking the conservation status of species. Species categorized as "Vulnerable" are those likely to become Endangered if factors contributing to their decline are not altered.

BIBLIOGRAPHY

Adams, Richard M., II. 1984. "Native Lilies." *American Horticulturist* 63(8):28-31.

Akerele, Olayiwola, Vernon Heywood, and Hugh Synge, eds. 1991. *Conservation of Medicinal Plants*. Proceedings of an International Symposium, 21-27 March 1988, held at Chiang Mai, Thailand. Cambridge, U.K.: Cambridge University Press.

Alabama Natural Heritage Program. 1992. "Plant Tracking List." Department of Conservation and Natural Resources, Montgomery, Alabama.

Allen, Oliver E. 1987. *Gardening with the New Small Plants: The Complete Guide to Growing Dwarf and Miniature Shrubs, Flowers, Trees and Vegetables*. Boston: Houghton Mifflin Company.

Arkansas Natural Heritage Commission. 1987. "Endangered and Threatened Plants of Arkansas." Department of Arkansas Heritage, Little Rock, Arkansas.

Art, Henry A. 1990. *The Wildflower Gardener's Guide: California, Desert Southwest, and Northern Mexico Edition*. A Garden Way Publishing Book. Pownal, Vermont: Storey Communications.

Arundel, Marjorie S. 1989. "The Smoking Trowel or the Last Minuet." *GCA Bulletin*. August 1989. Pp. 6-9.

Bechtel, Helmut, Phillip Cribb, and Edmond Launert. 1992. *The Manual of Cultivated Orchid Species*. 3rd edition. Cambridge, Massachusetts: The MIT Press.

Blumer, Karen. 1990. *Long Island Native Plants for Landscaping: A Sourcebook*. Brookhaven, New York: Growing Wild Publications.

Brandywine Conservancy, Mt. Cuba Center, and New England Wild Flower Society. 1990. *North American Native Terrestrial Orchid Propagation and Production*. Proceedings from a Conference held March 10-11, 1989, at the Brandywine River Museum of the Brandywine Conservancy.

Bratton, Susan Power. 1985. "Effects of Disturbance by Visitors on Two Woodland Orchid Species in Great Smoky Mountains National Park, USA." *Biological Conservation* 31:211-227.

Brickell, Christopher, and Fay Sharman. 1986. *The Vanishing Garden: A Conservation Guide to Garden Plants*. London: John Murray in association with the Royal Horticultural Society.

Bryan, John E. 1989. *Bulbs: Volume I, A-H; Volume II, I-Z*. Portland, Oregon: Timber Press.

California Endangered Plant Project. 1988. *Endangered Plants of California*. California Department of Fish and Game, Sacramento, California.

California Department of Fish and Game. 1992. "Designated Endangered, Threatened or Rare Plants and Candidates with Official Listing Dates, January 1992." Endangered Plant Program, Natural Heritage Division, Department of Fish and Game, Sacramento, California.

Case, Frederick W. Jr. 1990. "The Beloved Trillium." *Michigan Natural Resources*. May/June 1990. Pp. 4-11.

————. 1964. *Orchids of the Western Great Lakes Region*. Cranbrook Institute of Science, Bloomfield, Michigan.

Center for Plant Conservation. 1992. *1992 Plant Conservation Directory*. Center for Plant Conservation, Missouri Botanical Garden, St. Louis, Missouri.

Cheers, Gordon. 1983. *Carnivorous Plants*. Victoria, Australia: Carnivor and Insectivor Plants.

Chown, Marcus. 1985. "Rare Plants Piled High and Sold Cheap." *New Scientist*, 7 March 1985. P. 10.

Clausen, Ruth Rogers, and Nicolas H. Ekstrom. 1989. *Perennials for American Gardens*. New York: Random House.

Colorado Natural Areas Program. 1991. "Colorado Plant Species of Special Concern — April 1991." Colorado Natural Areas Program, Division of Parks and Outdoor Recreation, Denver, Colorado.

Connecticut Department of Environmental Regulation. 1991. "Endangered and Threatened Species, and Species of Special Concern." Department of Environmental Regulation, State of Connecticut.

Cook, Jack. 1990. "Allium underground." *Organic Gardening*. November 1990. Pp. 28-33.

Coombs, Sarah V. 1936. *South African Plants for American Gardens*. New York: Frederick A. Stokes Co.

Cornell University, Staff of L.H. Bailey Hortorium. 1976. *Hortus Third*. New York: Macmillan.

Cowley, Jill. 1989. "Allium virgunculae." *The Kew Magazine* 6(2): 61-64.

Cribb, Phillip. 1987. *The Genus Paphiopedilum*. A Kew Magazine Monograph. The Royal Botanic Gardens, Kew, in association with Collingridge, Middlesex, England.

——— and Christopher Bailes. 1989. *Hardy Orchids: Orchids for the Garden and Frost-free Greenhouse*. London: Christopher Helm, and Portland, Oregon: Timber Press.

Davies, Paul, Jenne Davies, and Anthony Huxley. 1988. *Wild Orchids of Britain and Europe*. London: Hogarth Press.

Davis, Stephen D. et al. 1986. *Plants in Danger: What Do We Know?* Gland, Switzerland and Cambridge, United Kingdom: International Union for Conservation of Nature and Natural Resources.

de Klemm, Cyrille. 1990. *Wild Plant Conservation and the Law*. IUCN Environmental Policy and Law Paper no. 24. Gland, Switzerland: IUCN-The World Conservation Union.

Delaware Natural Heritage Inventory. 1992. "Plants of Special Concern." Delaware Natural Heritage Program, Dover, Delaware.

DeWolf, Gordon P. 1990. "Knowing and Growing Bulbs." *Horticulture*. July 1990. Pp. 41-49.

Dressler, Robert L. 1981. *The Orchids: Natural History and Classification*. Cambridge, Massachusetts: Harvard University Press.

Duke, James A. 1986. *Handbook of Northeastern Indian Medicinal Plants*. Lincoln, Massachusetts: Quarterman Publications.

Dunn, Barbara. 1990. "Flypaper Trap." *Texas Parks and Wildlife*. February, 1990.

Ekim, T., et al. 1989. "List of Rare, Threatened and Endemic Plants in Turkey Prepared according to IUCN Red Data Book Categories." Turkish Association for Conservation of Nature and Natural Resources (Series no. 18), Ankara, Turkey.

Ekim. T. et al. 1984. "Taxonomic and Ecological Investigations on the Economic Geophytes of Turkey." Unpublished.

Falk, Donald A., and Kent E. Holsinger, eds. 1991. *Genetics and Conservation of Rare Plants*. New York: Oxford University Press.

Fell, Derek. 1989. *Essential Bulbs: The 100 Best for Design and Cultivation*. New York: Crescent Books.

Feltwell, John. 1987. *The Naturalist's Garden*. London: Ebury Press.

Ferenc, Németh and Seregélyes Tibor. N.d. *Save the Wild Flowers: Some Rarities Growing in Hungary*. Budapest, Hungary: National Environment and Nature Conservancy Office.

Florida Natural Areas Inventory. 1990. "Special Plant and Lichen List." Department of Natural Resources and The Nature Conservancy, Tallahassee, Florida.

Folkerts, George W. 1982. "The Gulf Coast Pitcher Plant Bogs." *American Scientist* 70(3):260-267.

Foster, Steven and James A. Duke. 1990. *A Field Guide to Medicinal Plants: Eastern and Central North America*. Peterson Field Guide Series 40. Boston: Houghton Mifflin Company.

Freeman, C. 1987. "List of Kansas Element Plants." Kansas Natural Heritage Program, Kansas Biological Survey, University of Kansas, Lawrence, Kansas. (updated periodically.)

Fuller, Douglas. 1991. *Medicine from the Wild: An Overview of the U.S. Native Medicinal Plant Trade and Its Conservation Implications*. Washington, D.C.: World Wildlife Fund.

Georgia Department of Natural Resources. 1991. "Georgia's Protected Plants." Ed. of 13 August 1991. Freshwater Wetlands and Heritage Inventory Program, Social Circle, Georgia.

Grey Wilson, Christopher. 1988. *The Genus Cyclamen*. A Kew Magazine Monograph. The Royal Botanic Gardens, Kew, in association with Christopher Helm and Timber Press, Portland, Oregon.

——— and Brian Mathew. 1981. *Bulbs: The Bulbous Plants of Europe and Their Allies*. London: William Collins Sons and Co.

Gupton, Oscar W., and Fred C. Swope. 1986. *Wild Orchids of the Middle Atlantic States*. Knoxville, Tennessee: University of Tennessee Press.

Hagan, Patti. 1991. "Gardening: Save the Wildflowers." *The Wall Street Journal*. November 19, 1991.

———. 1991. "Truth in Gardening: Uprooting the Black-Market Bulbs." *The Wall Street Journal*. January 3, 1991.

Harriman, Sarah. 1977. *The Book of Ginseng*. New York: Pyramid Press.

Hausman, Ethel Hinckley. 1947. *The Illustrated Encyclopedia of American Wild Flowers*. New York: Garden City Publishing Co.

Herkert, James R., editor. 1991. *Endangered and Threatened Species of Illinois: Status and Distribution, Volume 1 —Plants*. Springfield, Illinois: Illinois Endangered Species Protection Board.

Hobhouse, Henry. 1985. *Seeds of Change*. New York: Harper & Row.

Hodgson, Larry. 1989. "A Walk on the Wild Side: Naturalizing Bulbs." *Harrowsmith*. September/October 1989. Pp. 54-63.

Horticultural Research Institute. 1987. *Research Summary: Scope V of the Nursery Industry*. Washington, D.C.: Horticultural Research Institute.

Huxley, Anthony. 1985. *Green Inheritance*. Garden City, New York: Anchor Press/Doubleday.

Houtcooper, Wayne C., David J. Ode, John A. Pearson, and George M. Vandell III. 1985. "Rare Animals and Plants of South Dakota." *Prairie Naturalist* 17(3):143-165.

Indiana Department of Natural Resources. 1990. *Indiana's Rare Plants and Animals: A Checklist of Endangered and Threatened Species*. Indianapolis: Indiana Department of Natural Resources.

Iowa Administrative Code. 1988. "Endangered and Threatened Plant and Animal Species." IAC 11/30/88, Chapter 77. Pp. 1-13.

Justice, William S., and C. Ritchie Bell. 1968. *Wild Flowers of North Carolina*. Chapel Hill, North Carolina: University of North Carolina Press.

Kentucky State Nature Preserves Commission. 1991. "Endangered, Threatened, and Special Concern Plant and Animal Species of Kentucky." Kentucky State Nature Preserves Commission, Frankfort, Kentucky.

Koopowitz, Harold and Hilary Kaye. 1983. *Plant Extinction: A Global Crisis*. Washington, D.C.: Stone Wall Press.

Kraft, Ken, and Pat Kraft. 1989. "Culinary Gold." *Garden*. September/October 1989. Pp. 25-26.

Lesica, P., and J.S. Shelly. 1991. *Sensitive, Threatened and Endangered Vascular Plants of Montana*. Montana Natural Heritage Program. Occasional Publication no. 1. Helena, Montana.

Louisiana Natural Heritage Program. 1991. "Louisiana Special Plant List (February 1991)." Louisiana Natural Heritage Program, Baton Rouge, Louisiana.

Ludwig, J. Christopher. 1992. *Natural Heritage Resources of Virginia: Rare Vascular Plant Species*. Richmond, Virginia: Division of Natural Heritage, Virginia Department of Conservation and Recreation.

Mabberley, D.J. 1987. *The Plant-Book: A Portable Dictionary of the Higher Plants*. Cambridge, U.K.: Cambridge University Press.

Maine Critical Areas Program. 1990. *Maine's Endangered and Threatened Plants*. Augusta, Maine: Maine State Planning Office.

Maryland Natural Heritage Program. 1991. "Rare, Threatened and Endangered Plants of Maryland." Department of Natural Resources, Annapolis, Maryland.

Mathew, Brian. 1987. *The Smaller Bulbs*. London: B. T. Batsford.

———, Noel McGough, Mike Read, Hans Peter, Maria Wertel and D. Onno Wijnands. 1988. Report on Investigation into Status and Cultivation of *Cyclamen* Species and Other Geophytes in Turkey, April 1988. Presentation to the CITES Plants Committee, Royal Botanic Gardens, Kew, 4 April 1988.

McMahan, Linda R., and Kerry S. Walter. 1988. "The International Orchid Trade." Pp. 377-392 in William J. Chandler, ed. Audubon Wildlife Report 1988/1989. New York: Academic Press.

Mellichamp, Larry. 1986. "Carnivorous Plant Culture in Holland." *Carnivorous Plant Newsletter* 15(1):12-18.

Michigan Endangered Species Program, and the Michigan Natural Features Inventory. 1992. "Michigan's Special Plants: Endangered, Threatened, Special Concern, and Probably Extirpated." Michigan Department of Natural Resources, Lansing, Michigan.

Mierow, Dorothy, and Tirtha Bahadur Shrestha. 1978. *Himalayan Flowers and Trees*. Tripureshwar, Kathmandu, Nepal: Sahayogi Prakashan.

Miller, Richard Alan. 1988. *Native Plants of Commercial Importance*. Grants Pass, Oregon: Oak, Inc.

Ministerie van Landbouw. 1989. *Teelt En Gebruiksmogelijkheden Van Bijgoedgewassen, Tweede uitgave*. Lisse, the Netherlands: Ministerie van Landbouw, Natuurbeheer en Visserij.

Minnesota Natural Heritage Program. 1986. *Checklist of Endangered and Threatened Animal and Plant Species of Minnesota*. St. Paul, Minnesota: Minnesota Department of Natural Resources.

Mississippi Natural Heritage Program. 1992. "Special Plants List." February 14, 1992. Museum of Natural Science, Mississippi Department of Wildlife, Fisheries & Parks. Jackson, Mississippi. Unpublished.

Missouri Department of Conservation. 1991. *Rare and Endangered Species of Missouri: Checklist*. Jefferson City, Missouri: Missouri Department of Conservation.

Morefield, James D., and Teri A. Knight, eds. 1991. *Endangered, Threatened, and Sensitive Vascular Plants of Nevada*. Reno, Nevada: Nevada State Office of the Bureau of Land Management.

Morse, Larry E., and Mary Sue Henifin eds. 1981. *Rare Plant Conservation: Geographical Data Organization*. Bronx, New York: The New York Botanical Garden.

Moseley, Robert and Craig Groves. 1990. *Rare, Threatened and Endangered Plants and Animals of Idaho*. Boise, Idaho: Nongame and Endangered Wildlife Program, Idaho Department of Fish and Game.

Murray, David F. and Robert Lipkin. 1987. *Candidate Threatened and Endangered Plants of Alaska*. Fairbanks, Alaska: University of Alaska Museum.

Nabhan, Gary Paul. 1982. *The Desert Smells Like Rain: A Naturalist in Papago Indian Country*. San Francisco, California: North Point Press.

National Wildflower Research Center. 1989. *The National Wildflower Research Center's Wildflower Handbook*. Austin, Texas: Texas Monthly Press.

National Wildlife Federation. 1992. *Conservation Directory: 1992*. Washington, D.C.: National Wildlife Federation.

New Hampshire Department of Resources & Economic Development. N.d. *Protected Plants of New Hampshire*. Concord, New Hampshire: Natural Heritage Inventory, Department of Resources & Economic Development.

New Jersey Department of Environmental Protection and Energy. 1991. *The State of New Jersey Endangered Plant Species List*. N.J.A.C. 7:5C. Trenton, New Jersey: New Jersey Department of Environmental Protection and Energy, Division of Parks and Forestry, Office of Natural Lands Management.

Norquist, Cary. 1985. "Savannas and Bogs of the Southeastern U.S.: Threatened Ecosystems." *Endangered Species Technical Bulletin* 10(9):4-5.

Oldfield, Sara. 1989. *Bulb Propagation and Trade Study: Phase II*. Washington, D.C.: TRAFFIC USA.

————. 1985. "The Laundered-Bulb Trade is a Dirty Business." *Garden*. May/June 1985. Pp. 2-4.

Ohio Division of Natural Areas and Preserves. 1990. "Rare Native Ohio Plants: 1992-93 Status List." Ohio Department of Natural Resources, Columbus, Ohio.

Ohio Revised Code. 1992. "Administrative Rules for Ohio Revised Code Chapter 1518: Ohio Endangered Plant Law." Ohio Revised Code, Chapter 1501:18-1; Chapter 1501:18-2.

Oklahoma Biological Survey. 1992. "Working List of Rare Plants in Oklahoma (unofficial)." Oklahoma Natural Heritage Inventory, Norman, Oklahoma.

Oregon Natural Heritage Program. 1991. *Rare, Threatened and Endangered Plants and Animals of Oregon*. Portland, Oregon: Oregon Natural Heritage Program.

Pennsylvania Natural Diversity Inventory. 1992. "Plant Species of Special Concern in Pennsylvania." Pennsylvania Department of Environmental Resources, Harrisburg, Pennsylvania.

Phillips, Harry R. 1985. *Growing and Propagating Wild Flowers*. Chapel Hill, North Carolina: University of North Carolina Press.

Phillips, Roger, amd Martyn Rix. 1989. *The Random House Book of Bulbs*. New York: Random House.

Polunin, Oleg, and Anthony Huxley. 1987. *Flowers of the Mediterranean*. London: Hogarth Press.

Produktschap Voor Siergewassen, and Bloembollenkeuringsdienst. N. d. *Bloembollen: Beplante Oppervlakten 1987/'88 tot en met 1990/'91*. 's-Gravenhage and Lisse.

————. N. d. *Bloembollen: Beplante Oppervlakten 1986/'87 tot en met 1989/'90*. 's-Gravenhage and Lisse.

Quinn, Carey E. 1959. *Daffodils Outdoors and In*. New York: Hearthside Press.

Read, Mike. 1989. *Grown in Holland?* East Sussex, United Kingdom: Fauna and Flora Preservation Society.

————. 1989. "The Bulb Trade — A Threat to Wild Populations." *Oryx* 23(3):127-134.

Reinikka, Merle, A. 1972. *A History of the Orchid*. Coral Gables, Florida: University of Miami Press.

Rhode Island Natural Heritage Program. 1992. *Rare Native Plants of Rhode Island*. Providence, Rhode Island: Rhode Island Department of Environmental Management.

Rix, Martyn. 1983. *Growing Bulbs*. Portland, Oregon: Timber Press.

Rosengarten, Frederic Jr. 1973. *The Book of Spices*. New York: Pyramid Books.

Rutman, Sue. 1990. *Handbook of Federally Endangered, Threatened, and Candidate Plants of Arizona, Spring 1990*. Phoenix, Arizona: U.S. Fish and Wildlife Service.

Schmutz, Ervin M., and Lucretia Breazeale Hamilton. 1979. *Plants That Poison*. Flagstaff, Arizona: Northlands Press.

Schnell, Donald E. 1976. *Carnivorous Plants of the United States and Canada*. Winston-Salem, North Carolina: John F. Blair.

Sivinski, Robert, and Karen Lightfoot, eds. 1992. *Inventory of Rare and Endangered Plants of New Mexico*. Santa Fe, New Mexico: New Mexico Forestry and Resources Conservation Division, Energy, Minerals and Natural Resources Department.

Slack, Adrian. 1986. *Insect-Eating Plants and How to Grow Them*. Sherborne, Dorset, U.K.: Alphabooks.

South Carolina Heritage Trust. N.d. Untitled Plant List. South Carolina Wildlife and Marine Resources Department, Columbia, South Carolina.

Sutter, Robert D. 1990. *List of North Carolina's Endangered, Threatened and Candidate Plant Species*, February 1990. Raleigh, North Carolina: Plant Conservation Program, North Carolina Department of Agriculture.

Taylor's Guide to Bulbs. 1986. Boston: Houghton Mifflin Company.

Tennessee Rare Plant Protection Program. 1992. "Rare Plant List of Tennessee, 28 February 1992." Tennessee Department of Environment and Conservation, Division of Ecological Services. Nashville, Tennessee.

Texas Natural Heritage Program. 1992. "Special Plant List." Texas Parks and Wildlife Department, Austin, Texas.

TRAFFIC(U.S.A.) . 1989. "Pitcher Plants Enter Trade." 9(2):7.

van der Plas-Haarsma, Minouk. 1987. *Cyclamen in Trade*. TRAFFIC Rapport Nr. 5. Zeist, the Netherlands: TRAFFIC-Netherlands.

Vermont Nongame and Natural Heritage Program. 1992. "Endangered and Threatened Plants of Vermont." Nongame and Natural Heritage Program, Department of Fish and Wildlife, Waterbury, Vermont.

Walters, S. M. et al., eds. 1989. *The European Garden Flora*. Volume III: Dicotyledons (Part I). Cambridge, United Kingdom: Cambridge University Press.

Walters, S. M. et al., eds. 1986. *The European Garden Flora*. Volume I: Pteridophyta, Gymnospermae, Angiospermae–Monocotyledons (Part I). Cambridge, United Kingdom: Cambridge University Press.

Walters, S. M. et al., eds. 1984. *The European Garden Flora*. Volume II: Monocotyledons (Part II). Cambridge, United Kingdom: Cambridge University Press.

Washington Natural Heritage Program. 1990. *Endangered,Threatened and Sensitive Vascular Plants of Washington*. Olympia, Washington: Department of Natural Resources.

Wells, James S. 1989. *Modern Miniature Daffodils*. Portland, Oregon: Timber Press.

West Virginia Natural Heritage Program. N. d. "State Element List: Plants." Department of Natural Resources, Elkins, West Virginia.

Wheelwright, Edith Gray. 1974. *Medicinal Plants and Their History*. New York: Dover Publications.

Whittle, Tyler. 1970. *The Plant Hunters: 3,450 Years of Searching for Green Treasure*. London: William Heinemann.

Wijnstekers, Willem. 1990. *The Evolution of CITES: A Reference to the Convention on International Trade in Endangered Species of Wild Fauna and Flora*. Lausanne, Switzerland: Secretariat of the Convention on International Trade in Endangered Species of Wild Fauna and Flora.

Wilder, Louise Beebe. 1936. *Adventures with Hardy Bulbs*. New York: Macmillan.

Wildlife Trade Monitoring Unit. 1991. *Review of Significant Trade in Species of Plants Listed on Appendix II of CITES: 1983-1989*. Cambridge, United Kingdom: World Conservation Monitoring Centre.

Williams, John G., and Andrew E. Williams. 1983. *Field Guide to the Orchids of North America*. New York: Universe Books.

Willis, J.C. Revised by H. K. Airy Shaw. 1973. *A Dictionary of the Flowering Plants and Ferns*. 8th ed. Cambridge, United Kingdom: Cambridge University Press.

Wisconsin Bureau of Endangered Resources. 1991. "Endangered and Threatened Species List." Department of Natural Resources, Madison, Wisconsin.

Wyoming Natural Diversity Data Base. 1992. "Plant Species of Special Concern." The Nature Conservancy, Laramie, Wyoming.

Young, James A., and Cheryl G. Young. 1986. *Collecting, Processing and Germinating Seeds of Wildland Plants*. Portland, Oregon: Timber Press.

Young, Stephen M., ed. 1992. *New York Rare Plant Status List*. Latham, New York: New York Natural Heritage Program.

Zhang, Jingwei. 1982. *The Alpine Plants of China*. Beijing: Science Press. New York: Gordon and Breach, Science Publishers.

Index to Plant Names